Practical Sailing

Practical Sailing

Practical Sailing
by Tony Gibbs

Up-to-date,
complete,
authoritative guide to
handling today's
sailboats in
fair weather and foul

OVER 250 ILLUSTRATIONS

HEARST MARINE BOOKS

NEW YORK

For Tish

20 19 18 17 16 15 14

Library of Congress Catalog Card Number: 70-172014

ISBN 0-910990-37-9 (Soft Cover Edition)

ISBN 0-910990-38-7 (Coast Guard Auxiliary Edition)

Contents

Practical Sailing

Part I: Getting to Know the Boat

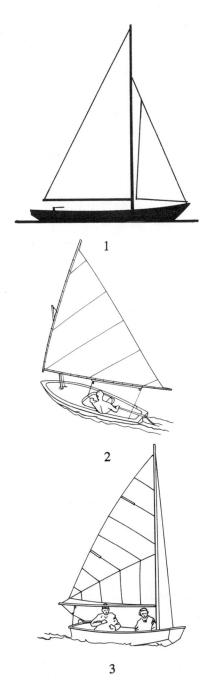

1

2

3

Today's sailboats vary widely in size and complexity, and it would take a bigger book than this one simply to list the currently available boats and their gear. But all sailing vessels work with the same wind and sea, acting according to the same principles on sails and hulls, and the essential parts of most rigs* are largely the same.

In this book, we'll be using as our running example a sloop-rigged daysailer (1), since that's a basic, two-sail design well adapted to learning and widely found in American waters. Most facts pertaining to sloops will apply to their cousins, the single-sailed boardboats (2) and dinghies (3), and their more senior relatives, the yawls and ketches.† The handling characteristics peculiar to other boats than sloops are briefly discussed in Chapter 19.

*(rig) *The standard arrangement of masts and sails in a given type of sailing vessel is her* rig, *which is also her type name—such as sloop, yawl, schooner, etc.*
†(yawls and ketches) *Common, two-masted rigs, usually seen in boats 30′ long or longer. See Glossary.*

1: Hull, Keel and Steering

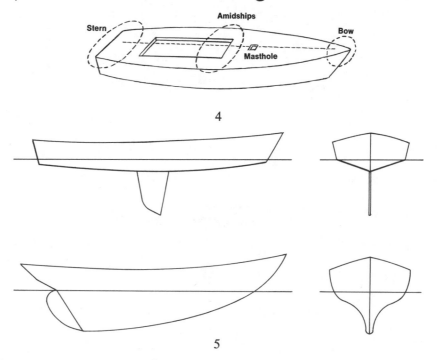

In becoming acquainted with any boat, it's a good idea to start with the hull—the most basic part, the container that holds the skipper and the crew, plus the vessel's operating machinery, be it engines or rigging. Hulls can be almost any shape, but most sailboat hulls look like illustration 4, because they're designed to do one thing: *move easily on and through the water in a single direction—ahead.*

Since water is harder to move through than air, the most important part of a boat's hull is what's under water when she's moving, the area below the waterline that comprises the boat's *wetted surface.*

Boats that move through the water are called *displacement* hulls, because they always displace a weight of water equal to the boat's own weight, while boats that are able to climb on top of the water's surface and stay there while moving—displacing only a fraction of their own weight—are called *planing* boats. While most fast power-boats are at least semi-planing types, even the fastest sailboats plane only in favorable conditions. When you stop to consider that a sailboat's planing is done without powered assists, what's surprising (as the man said of his talking dog) is not that sailboats don't plane better, but that they do it at all.

On land, the two best-known rigid containers are rounded bottles and rectangular boxes. The two most popular types of sailboat hulls correspond—*hard chine* (4) and *round bottom* (5). Neither one is absolutely better, and the following table compares their assets and liabilities:

HARD CHINE	ROUND BOTTOM
Easy to build in wood, hence cheap.	Requires more skill to build or repair, if wood.
Does not heel (tip) easily; but this great *initial stability* decreases quickly once the boat does begin to heel.	Heels easily at first, then increasingly resists further heeling.*
Has a less efficient under-water shape when moving while heeled.	Maintains a better under-water shape when heeled.

Many small sailboats are open hulled, but a boat over 12 feet or so is usually fitted with a deck (6), which not only strengthens the hull but also keeps a certain amount of spray and rain out of the boat, as well as providing a surface on which fittings may be attached.

The opening in the center of the deck is called the *cockpit*, and from it you and the

---

* Since stability is a function of beam, weight distribution and freeboard, a narrow, hard-chined boat could be tender, and a beamy, round-bottom boat could be stiff.

crew handle the boat. Water on deck is deflected from running below by the *coaming* (6), a ridge which runs around the cockpit's edge.

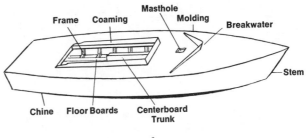

6

Keel and Centerboard

If you stand up in a small boat, it may well tip over: raising your weight has raised the boat's *center of gravity*,* making it unstable. A sailboat's spars and sails are a considerable weight; when the wind fills the sails, a small boat would be dangerously unstable without some counterbalancing weight below the surface, or a design factor (like broad beam) that inhibited excessive heeling.

On larger sailing craft, a deep keel with lead or iron weight at the lowest point provides stability. It also helps to keep the boat from sideslipping (the reasons why are in Chapter 6). But a boat with a sizeable keel has too much draft† for many sheltered sailing areas and is also much more difficult to launch, haul, or trail. Most smaller boats have, therefore, hulls with high initial stability designed in, and a retractable keel (called a centerboard or daggerboard) to prevent sliding to leeward.‡

The illustrations (7) show (a) a centerboard which pivots around the lower right-hand corner, and is raised or lowered by a pendant, and (b) a daggerboard which rides up and down instead of pivoting. The difference is that while either board may

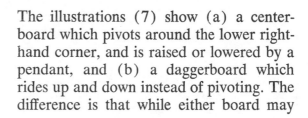

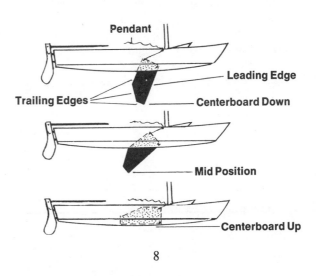

8

expose all, part, or none of its surface (8), the pivoted centerboard moves fore and aft as it's raised or lowered, while a daggerboard usually stays in about the same fore and aft spot, and changes only its draft.

Both boards are housed in trunks, strongly built and braced containers which may be capped in the case of a pivoted type, but

*(center of gravity) *Point in a vessel at which her total weight is considered to be concentrated.*
†(draft) *The depth of water required to float a given boat. Obviously a boat with a centerboard or daggerboard has two extreme drafts—board up (least) and board down (most).*
‡(leeward) *Pronounced loo'urd; the direction toward which the wind is blowing, as windward is the direction from which it blows.*

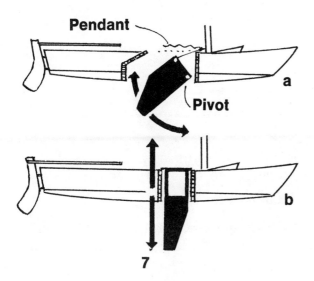

7

which is necessarily open at the top if it accommodates a daggerboard. The slot in the center of the hull, under the trunk, has to be wide enough to allow the board to move up and down freely, but not so wide that the board wobbles or twists. A wide slot also adds to turbulence and thus to drag. A wobbling board thumps as it moves from side to side, weakening the trunk, and it may also become jammed; it creates turbulence under the hull, as does a twisted board. The only cure for major centerboard trouble is a new board, a new trunk, or both.

Differences between these types of centerboards:

PIVOTED CENTERBOARD	DAGGERBOARD
Moves forward when lowered and aft when raised, pivoting on a pin. As it is adjusted, the *center of lateral resistance* (see p. 55) moves fore or aft, changing the balance of the boat. (Some daggerboards achieve the same effect through use of a diagonal trunk.)	Moves up and down, without a pivot, by hand alone. Can be difficult to work when boat is heeled, with strong side pressure on board. Longer and narrower (as a rule) than centerboard.
Trunk almost always extends into the cockpit, dividing it into two parts; trunk must be extra strong to withstand both strain of feet braced against it and stress on fittings attached to it.	Trunk placed well forward, allowing more room in cockpit: easier to brace into foredeck structure. Trunk is generally shorter, fore and aft, because it doesn't house the board in a horizontal position. Smaller underwater opening.
Requires a larger opening in the keel, creating greater underwater friction.	If the boat strikes an underwater object, it will jar to a halt, and the board and trunk may be damaged.
Will normally swing up undamaged if it strikes an underwater object.	Raised, the board gets in the way of cockpit fittings. Center of lateral resistance cannot be adjusted, because board moves only up and down.
Always housed or partly housed in its trunk.	

In the hands of a first-rate competition sailor, the centerboard is a vitally important device for adjusting the boat's balance; many casual daysailors will drop the board as they set out, and retrieve at the end of the day. There's a happy medium, which your own boat's reactions will determine. While there are few absolutes in centerboard handling, there are many generalities: the precise amount of board that should be exposed will depend on a combination of factors, including—

> weight and disposition of the crew . . .
> point of sailing* . . .
> hull form . . .
> and helm response.

*(point of sailing) *Attitude of the boat with respect to the wind determines her point of sailing; see Chapters 4, 5 and 6.*
†(headsail) *Any sail set forward of the foremost mast —jibs, forestaysails, and spinnakers are all headsails.*

Results include:

BOARD DOWN	BOARD UP
• aids steering	• makes steering more difficult
• helps keep boat from rolling	• decreases draft
	• changes helm balance
• reduces leeway	• increases leeway
• reduces speed (by increasing underwater friction)	• increases speed

A moment's thought will show that the board should ordinarily be lowered only far enough to maintain adequate steerage and reduce leeway. Some centerboard boats with several headsails† use the board adjustment to balance the particular sail combination they're using—an aspect of sailing that will be dealt with later.

Most new boats arrive with the centerboard faired off—the edges rounded or sharpened, the sides smoothed off—but when a factory has left the board (especially a metal one) rough, the owner should smooth it himself, to reduce turbulence and friction when the boat's moving. The illustration (9) shows several approaches to centerboard shape. A is best of the three; B is average; C is easily damaged, and is likely to cause flow separation at smaller angles of leeway.

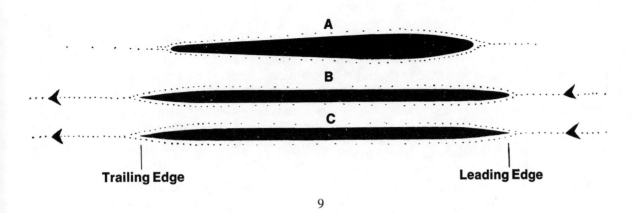

Trailing Edge   **Leading Edge**

9

Steering

A small boat's steering system is about as simple as a thing can be. It consists basically of one moving part—the tiller and rudder combination (10). When water is moving past the boat and the rudder is amidships,* pressure is equal on both sides of the rudder, which offers only a slight frictional resistance. Once the rudder—often hinged to the transom—is turned, water pressure builds up on the forward side and pressure is reduced on the after side. This uneven pressure forces the stern around (11), making the whole boat turn about its center of rotation—a point somewhere amidships. So a boat (unlike a car)

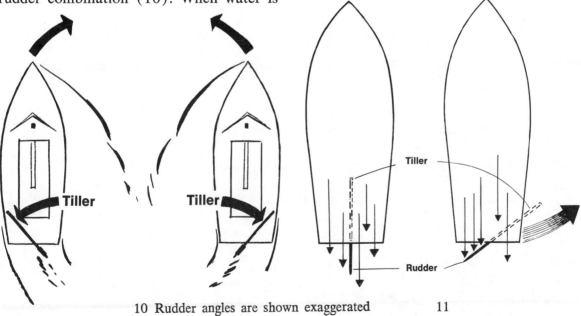

10 Rudder angles are shown exaggerated   11

*(amidships) *Usually, in the middle part of a boat; also used to mean a location anywhere along the boat's centerline.*

steers from its stern, not its bow: when estimating how your boat will maneuver, this is an extremely important fact to bear in mind, and something that becomes second nature.

A sailboat's tiller is simply a lever, to make moving the rudder easier; on a modern sailboat, properly balanced, the tiller is quite sensitive, and even a small motion can produce dramatic results. The boat's designer has specified the length of tiller he feels will provide good leverage for the rudder, when the tiller is held at its extreme end, and the helmsman will probably get the best results holding it there.

The tiller should be grasped as lightly as possible—in a well-balanced boat, fingertips will be adequate on some headings—and the boat steered with smooth, easy movements. Because the rudder brakes the boat when turned, the apprentice helmsman should school himself to work the tiller as little as possible: don't try to react to every small change in the boat's direction with a compensating rudder change. Allow the boat to feel her way among the swells to the best of her ability—which will differ with different boats.

As the diagrams show, *the tiller is always turned in the opposite direction from the one in which you want to go.* If you want the boat's bow to swing to starboard, push the tiller to port, and vice versa. Anyone who's operated a small outboard is familiar already with this fact of boating life, but people who've only steered with a wheel find it takes some getting used to. Once you find yourself handling the tiller without thinking about it, you're well on the way to becoming a good helmsman.

If your boat is equipped with a steering wheel, it works the same way as a car's wheel. You should also have an emergency tiller, and it would be wise to become familiar with its use, just in case.

2: Spars, Rigging, and Sails

In its simplest form, a spar is a pole that serves to extend a sail and keep it extended: *masts* hold sails up, while *booms* hold them out. A sailboat's mast and boom can be made of wood (usually spruce), but most boats seen today have aluminum alloy spars, because aluminum can be made lighter than wood for the same strength, and requires less maintenance. Some masts are made of fiberglass, and where controlled bending is desirable (see p. 55), 'glass is a very good material.

The illustration (12) shows a standard mast and boom with their associated hardware: for simplicity's (and your checkbook's) sake, it's a good idea to keep boat hardware down to what you actually need. Very few boats have been improved by second-thought gadgets, and the more holes you make in a spar, the weaker it is.

The most important single fitting on a mast is probably the halyard sheave—it is, after all, what makes it possible for you to raise

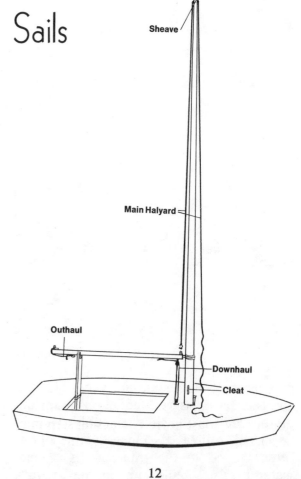

the sail. In our standard sloop, there are two halyard fittings: the main, which is usually a sheave recessed into the masthead, and the jib, which is most often a separate block attached to a tang* on the forward side of the mast.

There are a number of ways of attaching a sail to a spar, and the simplest is merely lacing it around, through eyelets in the edge of the sail. More advanced boats require that the sail tension be adjustable, and the two most common methods of adjustment use a recessed slot in the spar, into which the sail's edge is fed, or a raised track, which matches slides sewn onto the edge of the sail. Generally speaking, whether a small boat's mast uses a track or a slot, its boom will be similarly equipped.

Toward the base of the mast, a bit above the deck level, are the cleats† for the halyard tails and, in many cases, a winch or two. The winches are simply mechanical aids that enable the skipper to exert more tension on a halyard than he'd be able to with his unaided muscles; if your boat has only a single winch, on the port side of the mast, it's for the jib, not the mainsail.

trainers, have two mast steps, so the spar can be set forward or aft, and the boat sailed with reasonably good balance under mainsail and jib, or main alone.

To a certain extent, the boom's hardware parallels that of the mast. We've mentioned tracks and recessed slots already, but it's worth noting that some loose-footed sails are only attached to the mast and the outer

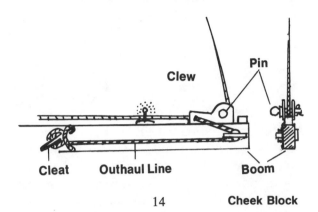

14   Cheek Block

end of the boom (see p. 15). Instead of a halyard fitting, at the outer end of the boom is a device called (reasonably enough) an outhaul (14). It can be a fixed block or one that slides along the boom track, but

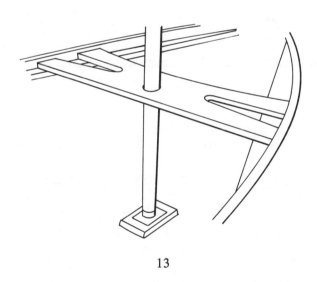

13

The foot of the mast may be *stepped* on deck or on the keel. In most decked boats, the mast runs through the deck, deriving some of its support from the close-fitting sides of the mast hole. The actual step may be a hole or it may be a raised fitting (13): in either case, it will match the foot of the mast. Some boats, usually ones designed as

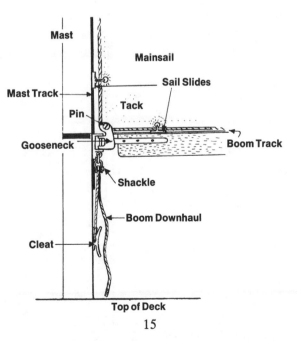

15

*(tang) *A light metal plate fixed to a spar, to which elements of the standing rigging are made fast.*
†(cleats) *Any of several devices used for temporarily securing lines.*

the purpose—adjusting the foot of the sail—remains the same.

The point at which the boom is attached to the mast is critical: a boom should be able to swing not only from side to side, but also up and down and diagonally. The universal joint that makes this possible is called a *gooseneck* (15), and it may be fixed to the mast or vertically adjustable, usually by sliding on a short length of track of its own. This latter arrangement, if available for your boat, is greatly preferable, as it allows much more flexibility in sail adjustment.

On gaff-, lateen-, and gunter-rigged boats (see p. 15), there's an additional spar for the upper edge of the sail. It's called the *gaff,* and it will be dealt with in a later discussion of types of mainsail.

The final spar commonly seen is the detachable *spinnaker pole,* which we'll examine in the chapter dealing with spinnakers.

Standing and Running Rigging

If the mast holds up the sails, what holds up the mast? In simple boats—and also in today's sophisticated boardboats—the mast is supported only by its step and whatever reinforcements may be provided by passing through the deck or a seat. A mast stepped like this can wobble somewhat, but it may be acceptable on grounds of simplicity.

As sailboat rigs become more complex, however, masts are subjected to simultaneous pulls and stresses from several directions. The old method of simply seating the mast securely is inadequate, and the spars are supported by a system of wires—usually stainless steel—called *standing rigging.* The ingredients of standing rigging are *stays,* which support the mast in a fore and aft line (16), and *shrouds,* (18), which support it on either side.

Diagram 16 shows a small, daysailing sloop; the jibstay runs from the bow or bowsprit* to a tang at the masthead, or to some point more than halfway up the forward side of the mast. (The masthead rig is more common in boats larger than the average daysailer.)

The standing backstay, on the other hand, always runs from the masthead, usually to a point at the extreme aft end of the boat, or to the corners of the transom, as shown. On boats that have exceptionally long booms, the backstay is led to a *boomkin,* a fixed spar (like the bowsprit) attached to the transom. Both bowsprits and boomkins are supported from below by *bobstays.*† Though not too often seen on sloops, double backstays are sometimes used.

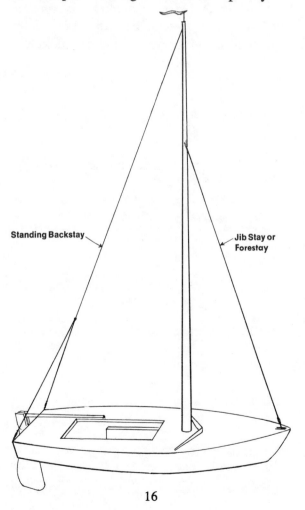

Standing Backstay

Jib Stay or Forestay

16

*(bowsprit) *A fixed spar projecting forward from a boat's bow; it extends the headsails forward beyond the bow.*

†(bobstay) *A wire, rod, or chain extending from the forward end of the bowsprit down to a stem fitting near the waterline. See illustration 17.*

Most small daysailers have a single set of shrouds; they lead from the rail or gunwale* abreast of the mast on each side, terminating at mast tangs level with the forestay tang. If a boat has no standing backstay—and many small boats don't—the shrouds often lead down to the deck slightly abaft the mast foot, to supply some support against the pull of the jibstay.

The next step in complexity calls for two sets of lowers, meeting below the spreaders and connected to *chainplates*† equidistant fore and aft of the uppers.

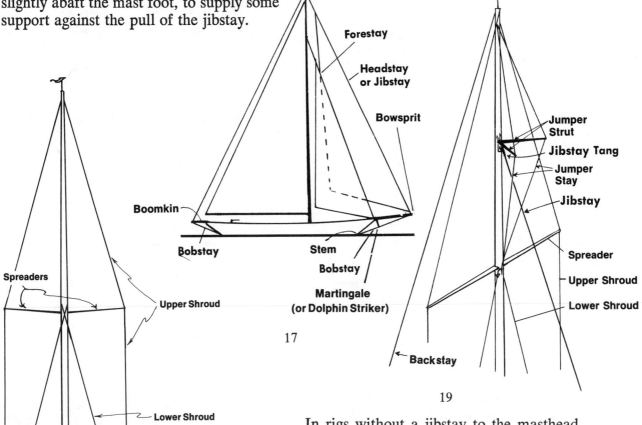

17

18

19

Medium-sized daysailers often have two sets of shrouds, called *uppers* and *lowers* (18). The uppers, which lead to the masthead from points abreast of the mast, have their supportive power increased by *spreaders,* small horizontal spars that hold the shrouds out from the mast and increase the angle at which they meet the masthead. The lowers go from points on deck slightly abaft the uppers and attach to the mast just below the spreaders.

In rigs without a jibstay to the masthead, and where a good deal of tension is exerted by jib and backstay, jumper stays are fitted to offset the uneven pulls: jumpers come in pairs, set about 45° on either side of the centerline on the forward side of the mast (19). The lower end of the jumper is made fast to a tang just above the main spreaders, the upper goes to the masthead, and the stay is "jumped" out from the mast by a small spar whose inner end is at the same height as the forestay tang.

All the standing rigging works together to form a cohesive supporting system. The proper fine adjustments for tension of stays and shrouds are made with *turnbuckles,* fitted at the lower end of a piece of rigging.

*(gunwale) *The upper edge of a boat's side.*
†(chainplates) *Metal strips well secured (usually through-bolted) to the hull of a boat, to which the lower ends of standing rigging are attached.*

Standing and Running Rigging 11

Running Rigging is so called because the rope or wire lines of which it consists aren't calculated to stand motionless but to run through blocks. Subheadings include—

halyards, the lines that hoist the sails,

sheets, the lines that control the sails once they're up,

and *lifts* (23), lines that support horizontal spars.

21

Each sail has at least one sheet; in the case of main and jib, the sheets lead back to the cockpit, and they may gain additional mechanical advantage from the use of deck or coaming-mounted winches (for jibs) (21), or block systems (for mains) (22).

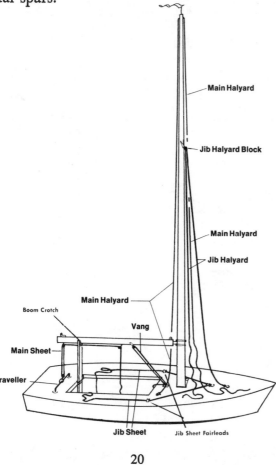

20

22

As noted above, sloops have two basic halyards, the jib and the main, plus a third one for the spinnaker, if that sail is carried. Halyards on smaller boats are generally made of Dacron, a synthetic line that combines strength, resistance to rot, and—to distinguish it from nylon—minimal stretch. But as boats get bigger, the stresses put on rope halyards are so great that even pre-stretched Dacron will stretch a small but annoying amount, and halyards are made instead of flexible wire rope with Dacron tails spliced to them—the wire for stretchlessness, the Dacron for handling. When a sail is fully hoisted, the wire part of its halyard should extend far enough down the mast to take at least three turns around the winch drum.

Sheets on all but the largest boats are Dacron, in either its *laid* or *braided* conformation.*

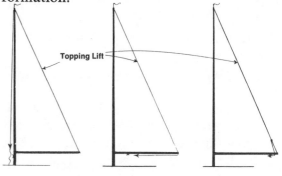

23

*(laid and braided) *See Chapter 26.*

Topping lifts (23) generally lead from the outer end of a boom to a masthead block, and then down to the base of the mast. They are lines which prevent the boom from falling into the cockpit when the sail is lowered. (See also spinnaker topping lift, p. 61.) Ideally, a topping lift can also be used as an emergency main halyard. Some lifts, however, are fixed at the masthead and are adjustable via the outer end of the boom. Whatever the method of adjustment, the function of topping lifts is the same.

Working Sails

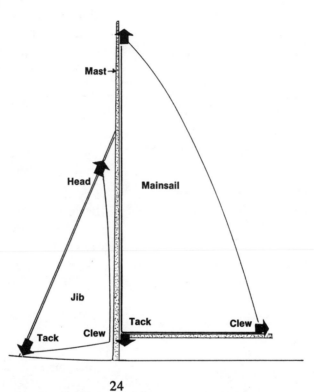

24

When men first began to sail, their boats presumably went only to leeward; the sails were square or rectangular, set from a boom-like spar called a yard.* Today's *Marconi* (also called *Bermudian* or *jib-headed*) rig (24) utilizes triangular sails that allow far more directional versatility, and the modern materials of sails, spars and stays permit great stresses on the sails and rigging.

The sloop rig's two *working* (i. e., basic) sails are of course its mainsail and jib. The principal parts of each sail, shown in the diagram, have the same names, which are important to know. The names of the sail's corners—*head, tack,* and *clew*—are frequently stenciled on the appropriate spot, so that a crewman pulling a sail from a bag will know instantly what part of it he's got. (Old-timers will sometimes confuse newcomers to the sport by referring to a sail as if it were a flag—calling its luff the *hoist.*)

Mains and jibs on boats of any size are almost always made of Dacron, which has in sails the same good characteristics it does in ropes. Both Dacron and nylon (which is used in spinnakers) suffer from prolonged exposure to direct sunlight, but they can be stowed wet without rotting.

All sails are built up from strips of sailcloth laid parallel to each other in one of several basic patterns; this pattern depends on the sail's use and the stresses which will act on it.

*(yard) *Any of several long, cylindrical spars, often tapered at the ends, used for extending square or lateen sails.*

Mainsail

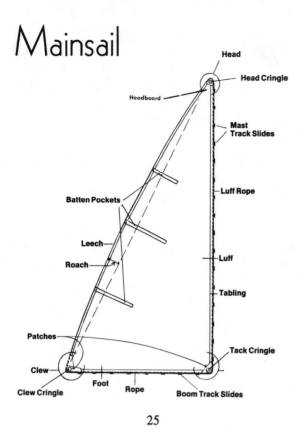

Head
Head Cringle
Headboard
Mast Track Slides
Batten Pockets
Luff Rope
Leech
Luff
Roach
Tabling
Patches
Tack Cringle
Clew
Foot   Rope
Clew Cringle
Boom Track Slides

25

Most mainsails use a pattern called cross-cut (26) for the arrangement of their sailcloths, with the strips laid at right angles to the leech. The mainsheet's pull comes at or near the clew, in a downward direction, so the stress is primarily across the seams and along the thread line of the fabric.

Along each of the sail's edges, and at the corners, is an extra thickness of Dacron called *tabling,* and along the luff and foot additional reinforcement comes from luff roping and bolt roping—line carefully stitched to the edge of the sail, providing support and also attachment to the spar, in the case of boats with recessed slots along mast and boom (26). Modern Dacron is, however, so strong that some sailmakers dispense with roping, and merely double or triple the tabling (hem) or add Dacron tape along the edge of the luff and foot.

A look at the mainsail diagram shows that the leech isn't actually a straight line: the edge forms an outward curve and the area between the leech and the dotted line is called the *roach*. Since this relatively un-supported area would sag or flutter by it-self, it's stabilized by thin, removable slats of wood or plastic, called *battens,* which fit into pockets whose open ends are at the leech. Battens should be a little shorter than the pockets containing them, and are held in by ties, specially-designed flaps or elastic-ended pockets that also keep them precisely in place. (27)

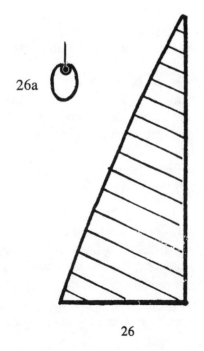

26a

26

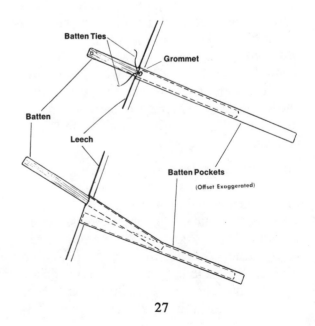

Batten Ties
Grommet
Batten
Leech
Batten Pockets
(Offset Exaggerated)

27

Dinghy and Sailboard Mains

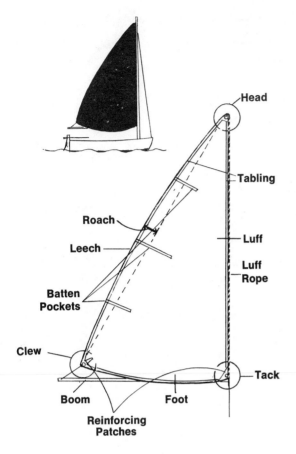

28

loose foot. The sail's long, main seam bisects the angle of the clew.

Loose-footed mains (p. 9) utilize a pattern of cloths called *miter-cut* (29). In addition to battens along the leech, there may be an additional one at right angles to the

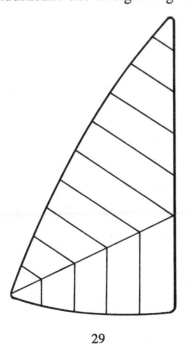

29

31

Besides the Marconi main, a few variants are in common use, most notably the gunter (30) and lateen (31) styles. A gunter-rigged main is usually laced to the boom and to a long yard which, with sail attached, is hoisted by its balance point to the top end of the short mast. A sliding gunter allows the lower end of the yard to be raised partway up the mast. Gunter rigs permit the dismantling and stowing of the spars inside the boat.

The lateen rigs on sailboards derive from an ancient sail plan that developed in the Mediterranean. It's similar to the gunter, except that yard and boom meet at a point slightly forward of the mast and pivot together around the mast.

The traditional pure gaff rig (32) has largely fallen into disuse: partly because of complexity, partly from lack of sailing efficiency, gaff riggers have reverted to the category of *character boats*—craft which often emphasize old-fashioned quaintness for its own sake. (33)

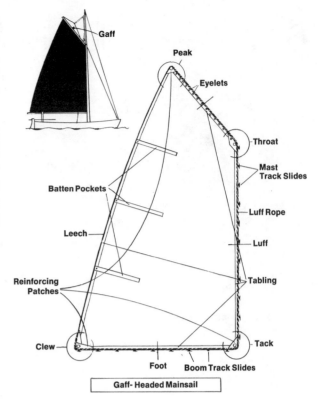

Gaff-Headed Mainsail

32

Working Jib

33

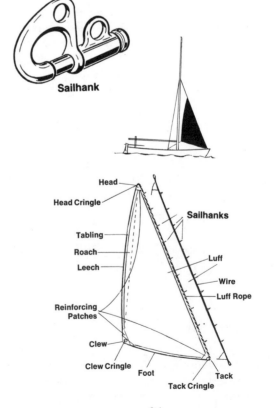

34

While the mainsail is extended and supported along two sides by relatively rigid spars, the jib is fixed only along its luff, which is snapped or otherwise attached to the headstay. The modern working jib occupies most (if not all) of the triangle formed by headstay, mast and deck. It may have battens along its leech, and its luff, where most of the stresses are applied in setting the sail, is frequently stiffened with a luff wire, to which the sail is sewn. In some cruising classes, the foot of the jib is stiffened by being laced to a club or boom or has its clew fastened to a pivoting boom (35).

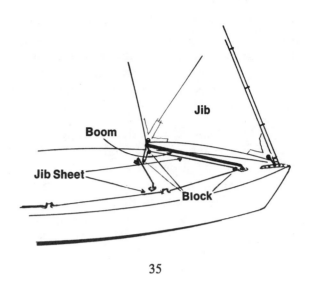

35

Part II: Under Way, Theory and Practice

Having assembled, in Part I, the various components of our standard sailboat, we will now leap from the drawing board clear out to sea, to discuss the general aspects of theoretical and practical sailing. But before dealing with the three points of sailing and the two basic sailing maneuvers, let's examine the wind itself, because knowing the wind's direction is vitally important to every sailor.

3: True and Apparent Wind

True wind is easy enough to define: it's the strength and direction of wind accurately recorded by an observer who is not in motion. But what you feel on your cheek in a moving sailboat (or a moving anything, for that matter) isn't true wind, but rather *apparent* wind—the sum total of the true wind and the "wind" created by the moving object itself.

For instance, you're standing on a pier and record a northerly breeze of five knots (winds are named for the direction *from* which they blow, i. e., a northerly blows from north to south, and are generally re-

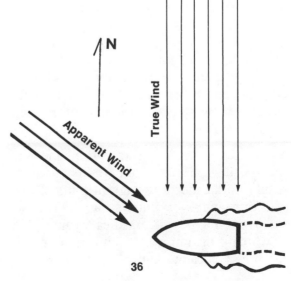

36

ported in knots). Aboard a nearby power-boat, moving due south at five knots, the crew will feel no wind whatever, because their boat's progress has cancelled out the wind. If they head directly into the wind, however, maintaining their speed, a man aboard will feel a breeze of ten knots in his face.

If the boat then changes direction again, so that it is moving at right angles to the true wind (36), the apparent wind will be coming from somewhere on the bow, as in the diagram. The important thing to remember about apparent wind is that (when your boat is moving ahead) it always comes from farther forward than the true wind, except when from dead astern.

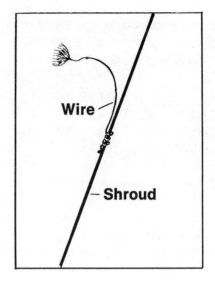

38

Wind vanes on shrouds are generally called *telltales*. Most skippers use ribbons or bits of teased-out yarn, but feathers (38) or special pivoting vanes are also available. When positioning any telltale, you should locate it so that it can't be wiped off by a

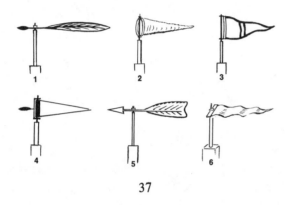

37

When apparent wind is forward of the beam, it'll be stronger than the true wind, because some of the boat's artificial wind is being added to the real wind force. When apparent wind is abaft the beam, it will of course feel weaker than the true wind.

You can't expect to get an adequate reading of the wind's precise direction simply from the feel of it on your cheek, and there are a number of wind vanes designed with varying degrees of complexity, from bits of ribbon tied to the shrouds up to tremendously expensive electronic indicators used on ocean racers.

Your boat's most important wind vane is at the masthead: it reacts only to the apparent wind, uninfluenced by vagrant puffs off the sails or rigging. The illustration (37) shows six popular types of masthead vanes, one of which is the burgee, which is more colorful, if less efficient, than regular vanes.

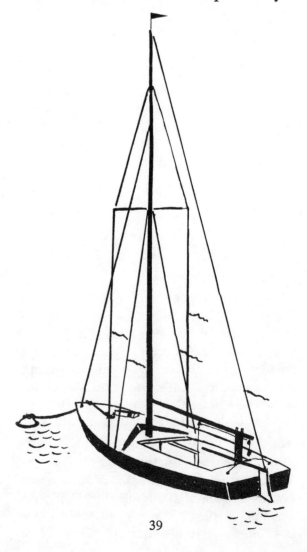

39

sail or sheet, or grabbed accidentally by an off-balance crew member (39).

Low-level telltales register the apparent wind as funnelled off the sails and rig, and may also catch tiny zephyrs at the water's surface; masthead vanes, on the other hand, react sometimes to winds missed by the lower indicators, especially when the hull area is blanketed by the shore or other boats.

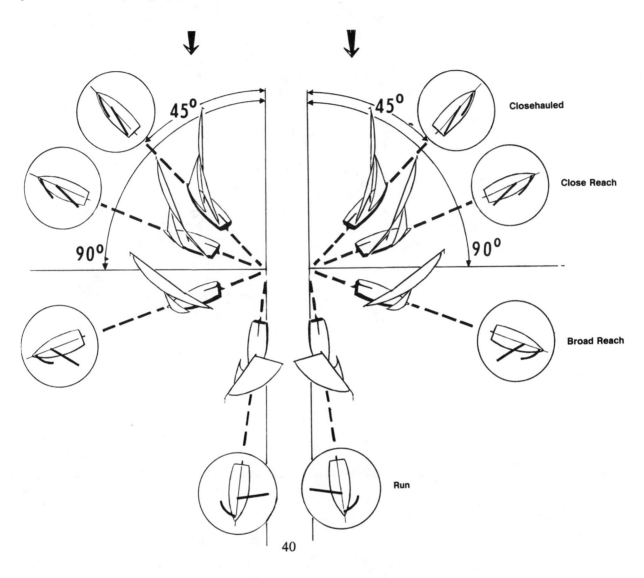

Closehauled

Close Reach

Broad Reach

Run

40

4: Running

While a modern sailboat cannot sail directly into the wind, it can point up to within 45° —more or less—of the direction from which the true wind is coming (41). Except, then, for the 45° on either side of the wind's eye, a well-designed marconi sloop can sail in any direction. Within this possible area lie the *three points of sailing*— the three general positions of the moving boat relative to true wind direction. These positions, which shade off from one to the other, imply different kinds of sailing, and they're called *Running,* Reaching,* and *Beating* (40).

---

* *It is easiest to explain the different points of sailing by beginning with running; in actual practice aboard a boat, it is most common to start with reaching and beating, leaving running to the last, when the student has aquired a little skill in wind reading and helmsmanship.*

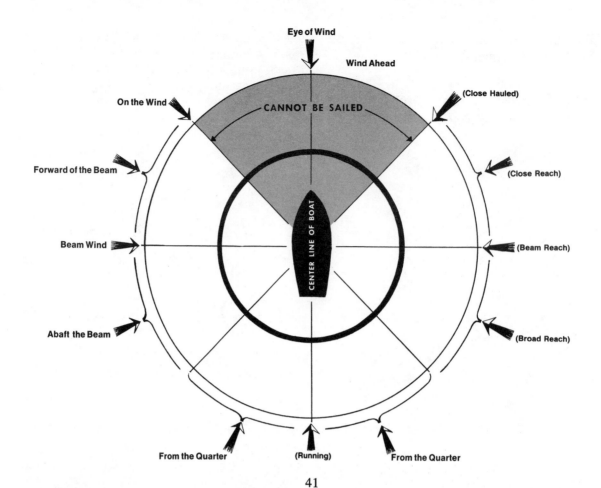

Eye of Wind

Wind Ahead

(Close Hauled)

On the Wind

CANNOT BE SAILED

(Close Reach)

Forward of the Beam

CENTER LINE OF BOAT

Beam Wind

(Beam Reach)

Abaft the Beam

(Broad Reach)

From the Quarter

(Running)

From the Quarter

41

42

Take running first, because it's the most obvious and understandable: when a sailboat runs, she moves in approximately the same direction as the wind, which comes from dead astern or slightly over either quarter. Contrary to what you might think at first, running is neither the easiest nor the fastest point of sailing for a modern boat.

A sailboat running has her mainsheet let out until the boom is nearly at right angles to the fore and aft line of the hull (42). The sail thus presents—in theory, anyway—a broad, flat surface perpendicular to the wind, and the force moving the boat is simply the direct push of breeze on sail.

Viewed from alongside, however, the sail is seen as not flat but curved: for one thing, the sail is cut so as to have a curve built into it;* for another, the boom is likely to be pulled upward slightly, resulting in a corresponding belly in the main part of the sail.

*(curve in sail) *By rounding the luff or foot of a sail, or tapering the cloths that comprise it: the book* Sails, *by Jeremy Howard-Williams, is the best current source of advanced information on sailmaking.*

43

The tiller may feel loose or dead, and more than usual tiller action may be required to produce desired changes in direction. The most important thing for the skipper to be aware of is the relative wind direction: as long as the wind is pushing the (more or

44

The working jib, which normally sets on the same side of the boat as the main, is blanketed* by it when running. It may be possible to pull the jib out on the opposite side, where, with good helmsmanship, it may fill and draw for a while: this kind of running is called *wing-and-wing* (43).

An improved method calls for the use of a spare spar, with one end made fast to the jib clew, to boom out the jib. Many small-boat sailors use a boat hook, while in some classes a *whisker pole* (44) is employed. At best, however, a boomed-out jib is a makeshift, and most boats employ a spinnaker for downwind sailing (see Chapter 18).

For a boat without a spinnaker, running can be tricky and dull at the same time. The boat is likely to feel sluggish and react slowly to the rudder; in light winds, she moves slowly and will seem to be moving even more slowly than she is, because of the reduced force of the apparent wind. Many otherwise skilled sailors consistently misread wind strengths when running, and are surprised by the force of the wind when they put the boat on another heading.

less) flat surface of the sail, the boat's in no trouble, but if the wind direction shifts slightly, or the boat changes her heading, the wind could get on the other side of the sail and swing it across the boat, just the way wind sometimes gets behind an open door and slams it shut.

When this happens—whether by accident or design—it's called a *jibe,* and while controlled jibing is an important and useful sailing maneuver (see Chapter 8), an accidental jibe is at best embarrassing (since it proves to all that the helmsman wasn't paying attention) and at worst dangerous, since the force of the swinging boom can seriously injure anyone standing in its path.

*(blanketed) *When one sail is directly leeward of another, and in its wind shadow, it flaps helplessly; it is said to be* blanketed.

5: Reaching

Let's say your boat has been running, with the boom on the port side. You head up slightly into the wind, taking in a bit on the main sheet, until the wind is on the boat's starboard quarter, and the jib (which had been blanketed by the main) begins to fill. You've just gone from *running* to *broad reaching* (see diagram on p. 19).

Suppose now that you head up still more, until the wind is coming at right angles to the boat (45a). The main and jib will luff (shake), and you respond by taking in on both sheets until the luffing stops. You'll try to keep from taking in anymore than necessary. Your point of sailing is now called a *beam reach*, and it may well be your boat's fastest heading.

Head up still more, until the sails are almost as far in as they'll go, and you're now sailing a *close reach* (45b). Note that you can still take in a bit more sheet if you have to.

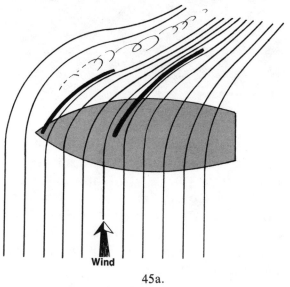

Wind

45a.

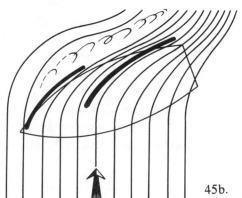

45b.

Close, beam and broad—these are the three types of reach, and of course they shade imperceptibly into each other, there being no precise point at which a voice announces, "you have just gone from a broad to a beam reach." Reaching is the fastest and the safest point of sailing, easiest on the crew and on the boat. Because it's easy, it's also hard to do really well: to get the most out of your boat when reaching, you have to be alert and ready to trim the sheets to every wind shift.

A boat reaching receives the same kind of positive, forward thrust from the wind as it does when running, but in addition it also benefits from the negative pressure peculiar to beating, which we'll consider in a minute.

While the wind's thrust broad on the beam of a sailless, flat-bottomed punt would cause it only to slide sideways, the combination of sail plan and hull design not only prevent slippage to leeward, but channel the force involved into a forward thrust (49) as explained on page 23.

A boat will heel as she reaches, and the closer to the wind she comes, the more pronounced the angle of heel will be. To set the sails properly for any type of reach, once the boat is on course, slack the main and jib sheets until the sails begin to ripple slightly along the luff. Now haul in the sheets slowly until the sails are asleep—

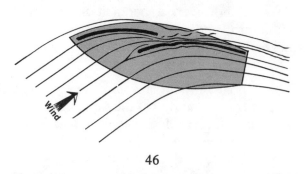

46

until, that is, the fluttering stops. With practice, only a few inches' trimming either way is required; trim the jib first, then the main, and be sure the jib isn't backwinding the main (46).

6: Beating

We left our example boat close reaching—her sails trimmed nearly as close in as they could be. Were you to harden in on the sheets until the sails were trimmed as closely as possible, meanwhile heading up until the boat was sailing as close to the wind as she could, you would then be beating, otherwise known as sailing *close-hauled* and *on* (or *by*) *the wind*. While a good 12-Meter, the paragon of yacht design, can sail within 35° of the true wind direction, the average daysailer can probably sail effectively to about 45° of the wind. The effect of apparent wind, especially in calm water with a steady breeze, will often make it seem as if the boat's sailing virtually into the wind's eye—but it isn't. But even sailing to within 45° seems impossible at first glance. How can a boat pushed by the wind sail against the force that's propelling it? The answer is simply that a sailboat which has the wind anywhere but astern is not being pushed by the wind, as one might expect, but rather lifted in the way an aircraft is lifted, by the action of moving air across the sail.

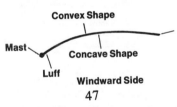

47

When a sailmaker creates a sail, he gathers, cuts, and sews the individual cloths so that the finished product, when filled by a wind, will have a curve like an airplane's wing—but vertical, of course, instead of horizontal. Though sails may be cut relatively flatter or fuller, all sails, regardless of shape, have a concave windward side and a convex leeward side (47).

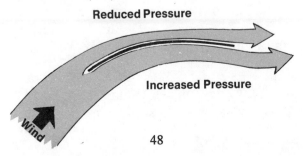

48

When a boat is sailing close to the wind, the breeze divides as it strikes the luff of a fore-and-aft sail (48): part of the wind passes over the windward side, part goes across the leeward side. The air flowing over the convex (or leeward, or forward) side of the sail has, obviously, somewhat farther to go than the straight line distance

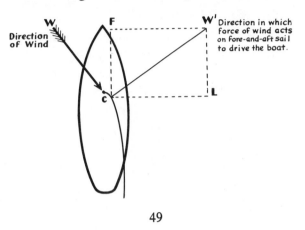

49

from luff to leech. The curvature of the sail speeds up the flow of air, and as a result a pressure difference is created across the sail, in turn creating a force which tends to move the boat in the direction CW^1 in illustration 49.

While this direction is a lot more productive than plain drift to leeward, it is not what we want. The force moving the boat in the direction CW^1 can be split into two components—a larger one, CL, producing leeway, and a smaller one, CF, producing forward motion. The boat's underwater shape is designed to maximize the effect of the forward component, while minimizing the effect of the push to leeward.

The more the wind moves aft, relative to the boat's heading, the greater will be the forward component of force, and the smaller the leeway-producing component. It's important when trimming sails to maintain the proper attitude of sail to wind, so that the maximum lift possible is achieved. When beating, it's not hard to see when the boat is stalled, but sometimes when you're reaching, your vessel seems to be going full tilt, when she would actually move better with the sheets eased.

In sailing to windward, your boat's jib is a very important factor. Not only does it furnish a certain amount of drive, deriving from the same principles that work on the mainsail, but it also channels air smoothly and swiftly across the mainsail's leeward surface (50), increasing the pressure reduction, and hence the sails' efficiency. That is, in fact, the jib's primary purpose in many sailing rigs, and so it follows that the relationship between main and jib is crucial in order to produce the most efficient *slot effect* between them.

Beating to windward, a boat's mainsail is hauled in just about as far as it will go (hence *close-hauled*), and the set of the jib is adjusted to make the proper slot.

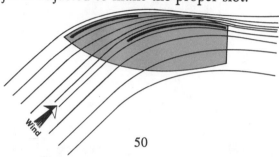

50

If the jib is pulled in too hard (or the main not trimmed hard enough), the mainsail is backwinded (see illustration, p. 77): the channeled air is forced against the mainsail's leeward side instead of smoothly across it, causing ripples that adversely affect the passage of air over both sides of the sail.

With the jib eased too much (51), the wind is hardly channeled at all, and the natural eddies toward the leech of the main's windward side aren't smoothed out. If the jib is

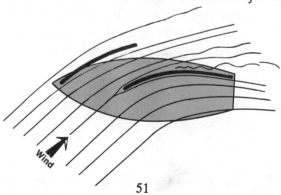

51

badly cut, so that it has a fluttering leech when on the wind, or even a hard curve at the leech, the same backwinding effect takes place.

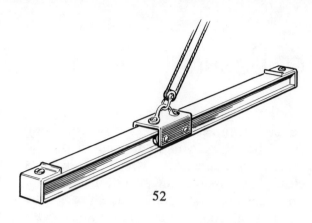

52

Trimming the main is also important, and the most vital adjustments are those involving the boom traveller: on most boats of any size, the boom's athwartships swing is controlled by a traveller—a car running along a track at the aft end of the cockpit (52)—to which the mainsheet is made fast. The reason for such complexity is that most booms are at the best angle for close-hauled sailing when over the boat's quarter, with the mainsheet pull close to vertical, to reduce the sail's natural twist.

The most important part of sailing to windward is keeping the boat moving well while as close to the wind as possible. The sails should always be full and drawing (except when it's necessary to spill some wind from one of them on purpose). Even when the wind appears steady, it's constantly changing, and the keen skipper trims his sails or varies course to every change.

When a boat points too high into the wind, the helmsman is said to be *pinching*: the boat's speed falls off, the sails begin to luff, and if the skipper doesn't *fall off*—turn away from the wind—quickly, the boat will lose all headway, with no drive from the sails.

On the other hand, if the wind shifts a few degrees from the bow, the alert helmsman takes the opportunity to head up or to slack sheets, whichever tactic gains the best advantage (see p. 30). This is called *playing the puffs,* and a good skipper can sail a *course made good*† that's far closer to the wind than that of his lazy buddy who sails by compass alone.

†(course made good) *The vessel's true progress over the bottom is her* course made good. *As opposed to the* course steered, course made good *takes into account the actions of tidal currents, leeway, faulty helmsmanship, etc.*

7: Coming About and Getting Out of Irons

So far, we've talked about sailing and changing *headings,* but not about changing *tacks*—that is, bringing the wind from one side of the sail to the other. There are only two tacks—port and starboard: a boat is on the *port tack* when the wind is coming from her port side, and her main boom is out to starboard. A *starboard tack boat* is taking the wind over the starboard side, and has her main boom out to port. The distinction applies no matter how much or little the boom is extended: thus a boat that's running is on one tack or the other, even though she may be dead before the wind.

It's possible to sail different headings within about a 135° range without changing from port to starboard tack, or vice versa. But of course involved maneuvering requires being able to change direction completely, bringing the wind's force to opposite sides of the sails. There are two ways of doing it, *coming about* and *jibing.* We'll discuss these maneuvers as they'd be done on a sloop. For cat-rigged boats, simply forget what pertains to the jib.

Coming about usually puts less strain on the boat's gear, and is hence the preferred way to change direction in heavy weather. It's simple enough to execute: when close-hauled on either tack, and moving well, the helmsman steers the boat up into the wind, continuing around until the sails fill from the other side, and the boat's heading has changed approximately 90°. The boat has now gone from close-hauled on one tack to close-hauled on the other, carried through the wind's eye by her own momentum (53).

Take it step by step. The boat is on the port tack, manned by the skipper and one crew member. The helmsman warns of his intention by giving the preliminary command, "Ready about." The crew, who's handling the jib sheet, gets ready to let it run free and stands by to avoid the swinging boom. When the skipper's sure that everything is in hand, he gives the second command—the command of execution, as they say in the service—"Hard alee" (or sometimes, "Helm's alee").

As he speaks, the skipper puts the tiller over to *leeward* in a single, smooth motion—neither a savage thrust nor a tentative push. As the boat answers her rudder, the bow swings up into the wind and the sails begin to luff.* This is the crew's signal to *cast off*† the jib sheet.

Still moving ahead, the boat continues to turn. As she does so, the luffing increases

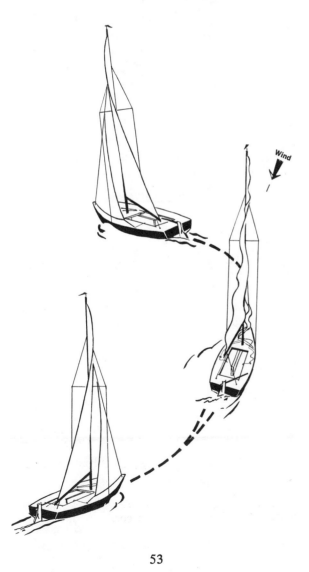

*(luff) *When the luff of a sail is no longer filled with wind and begins to shake, the sail is said to be* luffing. *When a boat heads up into the wind, she is also said to be luffing.*
†(cast off) *To untie and throw off a line from a cleat, winch, or similar fitting.*

53

until the wind is blowing with equal force across both sides of each sail. As the boat keeps turning, the sails—whose sheets are loose—swing across to the other side of the boat; the mainsail, whose sheet has not been released, fills with wind from the other side. At this point, the crew should haul in the port jib sheet (since the boat is now coming onto the starboard tack), to trim the sail. As the boat's bow swings through the wind's eye and the sails begin to fill, the helmsman eases the tiller back to its midships position, and the boat moves off. The tack has been completed.

Go back a few steps and examine a couple of places where the maneuver can go off the rails. What would happen, for instance, if the jib sheet had not been allowed to run when the jib luffed? As the boat swung through the eye of the wind, the jib would *back,* catching the wind on its reverse side and exerting a powerful leverage to swing the bow even faster—and an equally powerful braking effect, slowing the boat's forward motion (54). Some boats, especially ones with long, straight keels, are difficult to put about, and the jib is allowed to back for a moment or two, to encourage the bow to swing. But because of the accompanying braking effect, try to avoid backing the jib if you can.

At the other extreme is the over-eager crew member who begins to take in on one jib sheet as soon as he lets the other run. As can be imagined, this also causes the main and jib to work against each other, with the result that the boat will either fall back on the old tack or stall, refusing to settle on either tack—in which latter case the boat is said to be *in irons* (see below).

While the exact timing comes only from experience with a particular boat, in general it's a good idea to cast off the jib sheet a couple of seconds after the tiller has been put over—as soon as the jib begins to flutter. By doing this, the boat has the benefit of the jib's forward drive as long as it exists, and avoids the unproductive braking effect.

On racing sailboats, or those with crews and skippers who've sailed together often, the "Hard alee" command is frequently omitted: the crew knows that the skipper will call "Ready about," wait a second or two, and then put the tiller over. Beginning skippers may, incidentally, have an understandable reluctance to give commands to others, especially if they're such salty ones as *hard alee.* Just bear in mind that the crew doesn't know what's going on in your head till you tell him; and a mis-heard command is as useless as none at all.

If a boat is tempermental about coming about, it may be because of several things. A boat's performance may change according to the strength of the wind; in brisk winds and choppy seas, the boat may require a more forceful push on the helm, while in light airs, putting the helm over too abruptly may kill a boat's *way*—her forward momentum. In very slight breezes, the boat may simply not have enough way on to come about, and moving the tiller back and forth may add just the little extra speed to make it possible. This is called *sculling*, and in races it is illegal.

Another useful light air tactic is to let the boat fall off the wind a bit to build up extra speed, then begin coming about from a close reach.

54

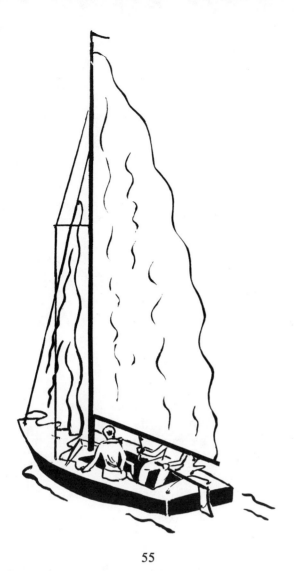

55

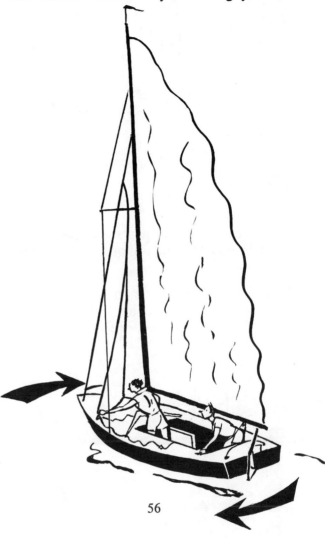

If this fails to help, take advantage of the boat's *sternway*, her tendency to blow backward. As the boat begins to move, back the jib *opposite to* the direction in which you want to go, while letting the main luff freely (56). The jib should be enough to swing the bow, but if it isn't try pulling up the centerboard. In a jibless dinghy, back

When winds are squally,* wait for a gap between puffs before coming about, to keep the sails from slatting destructively as they luff. In the same way, when seas are choppy, it pays to wait for a *smooth* between waves, and then come about quickly.

Sooner or later, though, your boat will fail to come about and will lie dead in the water, with the breeze blowing equally on both sides of the fluttering sails (55). This predicament, being *in irons* or *caught in stays,* is an embarrassing moment for skipper and crew.

The best way of getting out of irons depends to a certain extent on the type of boat you have. Small centerboarders are generally so well-balanced that a few quick jerks on the tiller will spin the boat off dead center and get the sails drawing again. What you've done is force the stern to turn slightly, presenting one or the other side of the sails to the wind.

56

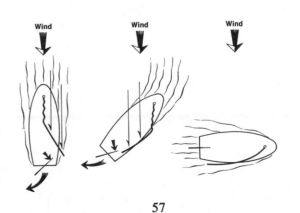

57

*(squally) *A squall is a sudden, violent gust of wind, often accompanied by a change in wind direction.*

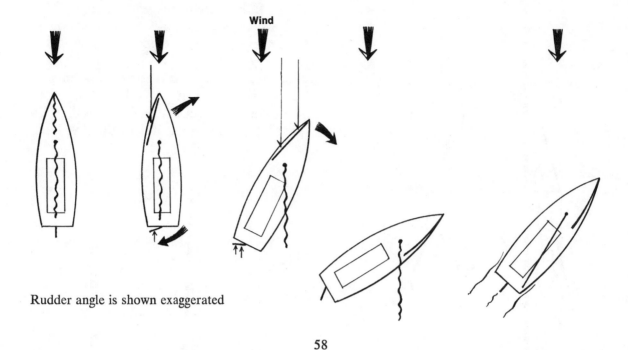

Rudder angle is shown exaggerated

58

the main as the boat gains sternway, then sail off when the wind is more or less abeam (57).

Heavy boats may have to be levered at both ends: put the jib aback and simultaneously push the tiller over to the other side (58).

And if none of these techniques work, simply slack the sheets and pull the centerboard up: the boat will slowly assume a position at right angles to the wind, at which point you drop the board, sheet home the sails, and sail away.

8: Jibing

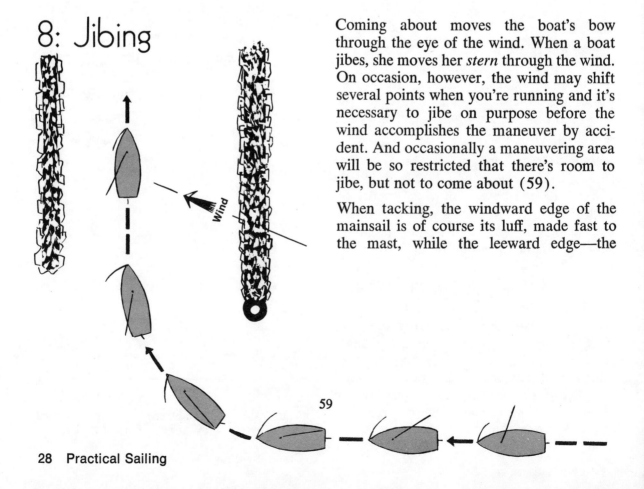

Coming about moves the boat's bow through the eye of the wind. When a boat jibes, she moves her *stern* through the wind. On occasion, however, the wind may shift several points when you're running and it's necessary to jibe on purpose before the wind accomplishes the maneuver by accident. And occasionally a maneuvering area will be so restricted that there's room to jibe, but not to come about (59).

When tacking, the windward edge of the mainsail is of course its luff, made fast to the mast, while the leeward edge—the

59

leech—swings free as the boat passes through the eye of the wind. Thus the sail is free to assume a neutral position, with wind pressure equal on both sides of the sail, from the moment of luffing until the sail fills on the opposite tack. In jibing, the windward edge of the sail is the leech, controlled only by the mainsheet, while the leeward edge—the luff—remains fixed.

This means that the sail cannot assume a neutral attitude to the wind while the boat is jibing—not for more than a moment, anyway—and the maneuver of jibing is less controlled, more abrupt, and more risky in strong winds than is tacking.

It is, however, vital to know how to jibe properly, and it's easy to do under most conditions. Here's how:

1. The boat is running with main boom fully extended (60). The skipper calls out, "Stand by to jibe." If the board has been raised for extra speed, it should now be partially dropped for extra control during the maneuver. If the jib has been poled out, remove the pole.

2. While maintaining course, sheet in the main as far as it would normally come when on a beat; stand by the jib sheet. Make sure the mainsheet is in a loose coil that's been capsized* to allow it to run out smoothly and quickly.

3. The skipper calls "Jibe-oh." He puts the tiller over, carefully, slowly, and *away* from the side the boom is on. As the boat swings, the wind will get behind the main and snap the sail and boom across the cockpit fast. Keep heads down. Shift the crew's weight to the opposite side of the cockpit, avoid becoming tangled with the mainsheet.

4. As the boom swings out on the opposite side, the skipper (or crew) should let the mainsheet out in a controlled run, with some tension on the line, stopping the boom's swing well clear of the shrouds. This is where incautious sailors get rope burns, and you may be well advised to wear gloves until your palms become calloused. Put the tiller amidships, trim the jib as required, and raise the board. The boat is on her new course.

*(capsized) *To turn something upside down is to capsize it: a capsized coil is one in which the unattached end is at the bottom and the working end at the top, free to run.*

Always harden in the sail before beginning the actual jibe, except in very light airs, when it may be simpler to haul the mainsheet in hand over hand.*

As noted earlier, accidental jibes can be very dangerous, though they are usually harder on the nerves than on the rigging. A wildly-swinging boom can hit someone on the head—and even knock him overboard; it may rise and foul the backstay (61), swing hard enough to damage the shrouds, or even dismast the boat; the uncontrolled mainsheet may foul itself, some piece of equipment, or a member of the crew.

*(hand over hand) *A multi-part tackle, like most mainsheets, offers the sailor mechanical advantage in return for reduced speed of hauling. By grasping all parts of the sheet at once, without allowing the line to run through its blocks, you can haul a sheet much faster—but without any mechanical advantage.*

61

9: Sailing a Course

To get from place to place—even if it's only a straight line between buoys—the skipper chooses among all the maneuvers at his command and picks the appropriate ones. Yet sailing a course is a maneuver in itself, and is an achievement greater than the sum of its parts—a fact that's never more evident than when the destination is in the 90° upwind arc.

When this is the case, a boat reaches her objective by sailing a series of zig-zags, coming about at the end of each one (62). The maneuver as a whole is called *tacking* and each leg a *tack* (sometimes a *board*). If her destination is directly upwind, a boat will sail tacks of equal length. If the objective is to one side of the wind's eye, a combination of short and long legs may be best: for instance, if the wind is coming from your objective's starboard side, the

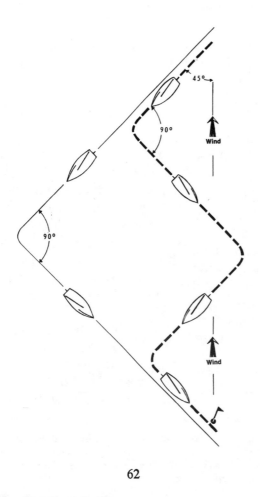

62

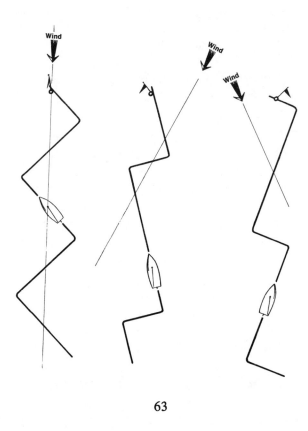

63

ables as wind and sea conditions and the skill of the helmsman.

While a boat makes leeway on every heading except dead before the wind, her leeward slippage is most pronounced when sailing close hauled or on a close reach. Every skipper should have a general notion of the amount of leeway his boat makes under varying conditions—the kind of operational information that can only be acquired by experience. It's also useful to know how much effect the centerboard has, and this can be estimated fairly accurately by sailing a predetermined course with the board down, and then sailing it again, immediately, with the board up (65).

64

longer tacks will be starboard tacks; and vice versa (63).

Since time spent coming about and settling down on a new course is time lost, long tacks are obviously more efficient than short tacks, because there are fewer of them. On the other hand, long tacks may be out of the question in crowded, constricted waters like anchorages. In sailboat racing, short tacking is a recognized tactic, and the winning skipper is often the man who can put his boat about consistently and reliably, without losing more than the minimum in way: even without the competitive spur, the same is true of the daysailer, who will find many more ways out of a given situation when he can rely on his boat's tacking ability.

Sailing a course close-hauled or in a series of boards* would be largely a mathematical exercise were it not for the fact of leeway—the inevitable slippage to leeward that every boat makes because of the side pressures on sails and hull (64). Each boat makes a certain amount of leeway, depending not only on fixed factors like hull and sail design, but also on such vari-

*(board) *Another word for the noun* tack.

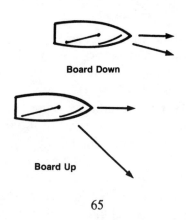

Board Down

Board Up

65

The variation in leeway made and in the boat's angle of heel between board down and up may be surprising; as the wind gets stronger and the water choppier, leeway becomes more pronounced, even with the board fully lowered.

Most small boat skippers sail within sight of land, and if there's no current, it's not hard to check one's leeway by sighting on two fixed objects in line ahead of you. If they stay in line, forming what sailors call a *range*, then the boat's course over the bottom is the same as her heading. If they move apart, the boat is making leeway.

Or check the boat's wake astern, if there aren't any handy landmarks. If the wake is an extension of the boat's centerline, there's little or no leeway. If it forms an angle with the centerline, that angle represents your leeway.

Most mistakes in tacking along a course come on the final board or leg. Optimistic skippers come about for the last tack too

66

67

soon, neglecting leeway, and fall short of the mark. Overcautious sailors tack too late, and waste time overstanding the mark.* If one is going to make any error, it's obviously better to hold to one's course for a few extra seconds and be sure of laying the mark on the final tack.

One way of telling how the boat stands in relation to her objective is to face forward, extend one arm sideways, perpendicular to the boat's course, and sight the mark along it (67). Until the mark is at least abeam, there's little or no reason to come about for the final tack.

This discussion of leeway is, of course, concerned only with the boat's leeway moving through the water. A current will obviously set any boat to one side or the other, forward or back, increasing or offsetting the boat's leeway and/or speed (68). The clever skipper learns what currents operate in his waters and when, and uses them to the best advantage.

Sailing a course downwind, the skipper doesn't have to worry so much about making leeway, but in rough or windy weather, he may find it safer to tack downwind, especially if his objective is directly to leeward.

To do this, simply lay a course that's a series of broad reaching zig-zags, thus keeping the wind safely on the quarter. At the end of each leg, instead of jibing, bring the boat around in a circle and come about. In racing, the term "tacking downwind" is used to describe a tactic that actually involves a series of jibes from one side to the other on a downwind run.

*(overstanding the mark) *To sail a course made good that is further to windward than necessary causes a boat to* overstand *the mark—to finish the course further to windward than you had to.*

Wind

Current

Wind

68

10: Angle of Heel and Stability

When a powerboat heels, the skipper knows something's wrong and takes steps to correct it. This isn't necessarily true of a sailboat: some small sailing craft can actually improve their performance by heeling as much as 30° off vertical. Beyond that point, the hull shape begins to retard the boat's speed through the water.

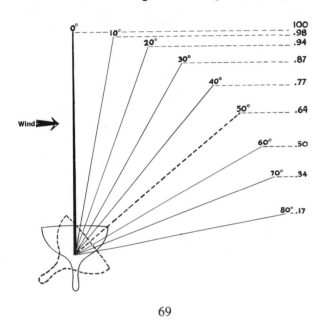

69

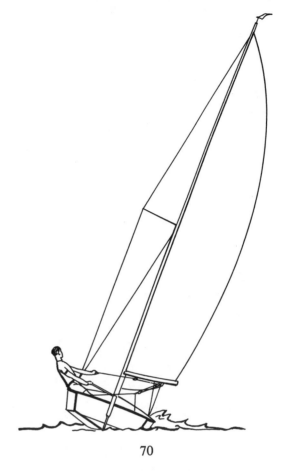

70

and the boat herself is in danger of being knocked down.*

The accompanying chart shows how the effective sail area of a boat decreases as she heels (69). Between 0° and 10°, only 2% of the effective sail area is lost, as compared to 13% between 40° and 50°, the critical angle of heel indicated by the dotted line. To some extent, then, heeling is a safety factor, since it reduces the exposed sail area; but at 50° of heel, even though the sail's effective area is down to 64%, the boat is on the verge of knockdown or capsize.

In a small boat, the crew's weight is a significant fraction of the boat's weight, and the crew controls the angle of heel by moving themselves from side to side. Under normal sailing conditions, the boat heels somewhat to leeward, and the crew partially compensate by sitting on the windward side.

As the wind pipes up stronger, the crew may have to hike out to windward to keep the boat on her feet (70). Note the tiller extension, used to allow the helmsman to hike out and steer effectively at the same time (71). If hiking out doesn't work, then wind must be spilled by luffing or the sail area reduced by reefing (see Chapter 21).

When the wind is too feeble to heel the boat alone, the crew purposely heel their vessel by moving to the leeward side of the cockpit (72). This forces the sails to lie over on the leeward side and assume their proper curve, so that what air there is will flow naturally over them, imparting the maximum drive under the circumstances. This type of imposed heeling shouldn't exceed about 10°.

In light and medium winds, the crew should avoid unnecessary moving about,

* (knocked down) *When a boat heels to the point that her rudder and centerboard come up out of the water, she is out of control and may be capsized.*

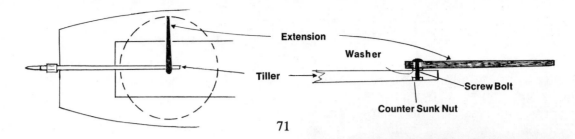

Extension

Washer

Tiller

Screw Bolt

Counter Sunk Nut

71

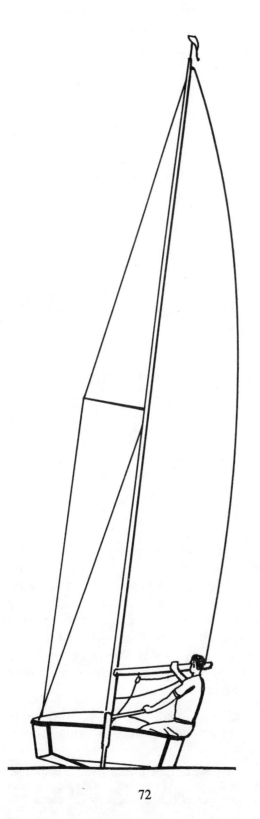

72

73

74

as sudden movements tend to jar the wind from the sails and impede the boat's momentum.

In the strongest winds, crews may lie along the weather rail, with one arm and one leg outboard (73), or they may use hiking straps (74), which (when coupled with strong stomach muscles) allow the crew weight to exert great leverage.

Part III: Basic Boat Handling

Thanks in part to trailer boating and dry sailing,* boat handling now includes rigging and stepping the mast, as well as maneuvering under sail. Just as handling a car in city traffic is harder work than driving it down a highway, close-quarters handling, especially in the vicinity of other boats, can be very tricky for the novice sailboat skipper. All the handling techniques we'll discuss in the following section should be practiced over and over, preferably in an area far from other craft and certainly out of the way of harbor traffic.

You may feel mildly foolish powering or paddling to a quiet spot for practice, but until you can handle your boat confidently in a crowded anchorage, you're far safer away from other boats. In the mooring and unmooring exercises we'll deal with, make a temporary mooring using a cushion or plastic detergent bottle for a buoy. An inflatable swimming mattress, with a small anchor, makes a good simulated pier— and it won't mar your boat if you hit it, either.

*(dry sailing) *A boat stored ashore, instead of being docked or moored, when not sailing is said to be* dry-sailed. *This is usually done for racing craft, in order to prevent marine growths from forming below the waterline, thus slowing the boat.*

11: Rigging the Boat

While boats that lie at moorings* between voyages usually leave their masts stepped, boats that reach the water on a trailer have to set up the mast and rigging for each sail. It's not hard to do if you approach the job methodically.

If possible, step the spar ashore: this prevents the added difficulty of standing up and moving about in an unstable small boat. While a single reasonably strong teenager can step a dinghy mast, installing the main spar of a 16- or 20-foot daysailer requires two people for ease and safety. The boom is, of course, not attached until the mast has been stepped.

First, gather the shrouds and stays together, making sure they're not tangled, and tie them to the mast so they won't flail about; be sure not to tie them at a point higher than the crew can reach once the mast is stepped (75).

on his shoulder, while the other guides the foot through the hole in the deck (76). As the first man moves slowly forward, the mast is eased into place, rising slowly toward the vertical (77). When the mast foot is firmly on or in the step, it should stand alone, at which time the shrouds and stays can be sorted out and made fast to the chainplates. A small dab of paint on each turnbuckle will give the skipper a good idea of how many turns to take up for initial tuning. Lock the turnbuckles with cotter pins or rings and tape any sharp protrusions to prevent sail damage.

76

Caution: many small boats are not strong enough to withstand walking on them when hauled out as shown.

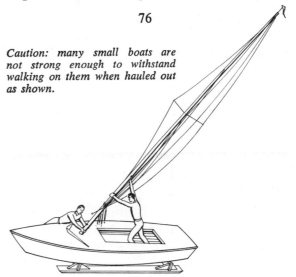

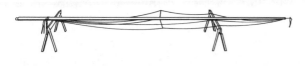

75

One man, standing aft, holds the spar— track side *down*—more or less balanced

*(moorings) *A semi-permanent anchoring system, often left in place for a full season, is called a mooring. See Chapter 15.*

Once the mast is set up, sight along the track to make sure the spar is straight, with no hook to port or starboard. Then stand off at a distance and sight directly over bow or stern, to check that the mast is straight in the boat. Depending on the boat, the mast may have been meant to rake* a bit—usually the exact amount is decided by experiment. On some sail plans

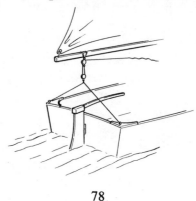

78

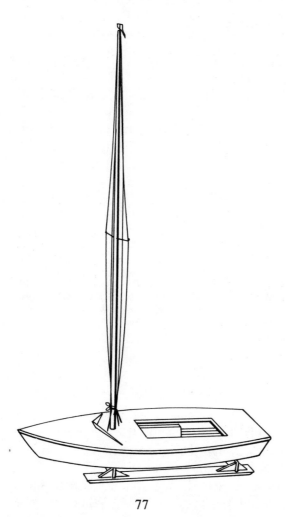

77

We'll leave fine points of tuning the rig for Chapter 16, but here are a few basics to note: fore- and backstays should be set up taut, the upper shrouds should be moderately taut, and lower just tight enough so there's no slack on either side when the mast is vertical. The precise degree of strain is a matter of trial and error, but it's better to start with the rigging on the loose side and tighten it gradually, bearing in mind that in most boats, the ideal is to keep the mast straight under all sailing conditions.

a particular amount of rake is specified by the designer. Now be sure to lock all turnbuckles with cotter pins or safety wire, then tape over any sharp ends.

Next, attach the rudder and tiller. If your boat has a wire bridle or raised rod traveller,** make sure the tiller is *under it*. (78). Make sure your halyards are clear.

Now make the boom fast to the mast, and attach the mainsheet to the boom. If your boat has a boom crotch,† rest the boom in its slot, but leave the mainsheet free to run once the sail is hoisted.

*(rake) *To incline aft (or occasionally forward) from the vertical.*
** (traveller) *A bridle, rod, or track on which the lower mainsheet block slides.*
† (boom crotch) *A rigid support, usually removable, that holds the boom horizontal and fixed when the boat is not in use. Also, "crutch."*

12: Bending and Hoisting Sail

Skipper and crew are ready to bend* on the mainsail, which has been neatly stowed (79) till now in its own, properly-marked bag. Most people find it convenient to stow the main with its head at the bottom of the

* (bend) *A sail is said to be bent on a spar or stay when it is attached, ready for hoisting. A* bend, *on the other hand, is a type of knot.*

bag and the clew cringle at the top, since this latter fitting is the one you'll want first.

Had the mast and boom been left up since the previous sail, the main halyard shackle would have been made fast to the boom outhaul. Now make the shackle fast to some point near the base of the mast.

Extract the foot of the sail, beginning with the clew, and slip it into the recessed track of the boom at the inboard end (80). Pull

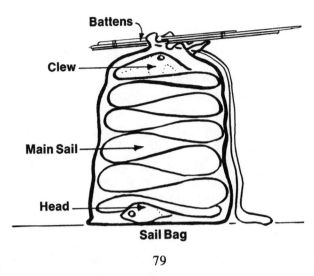

79

the clew along easily until it is almost to the outer end of the boom. If your sail is fitted with slides along the foot, make sure the foot is untwisted before inserting slides, so one doesn't go on backwards.

Now fasten the outhaul fitting to the clew cringle, and the tack cringle to the goose-

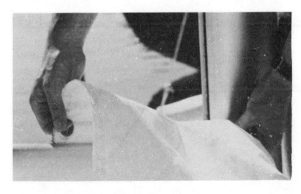

80

neck. The outhaul should now be pulled toward the outer end of the boom until the foot of the sail is hand taut.

Release the halyard shackle from whatever it had been made fast to, and extend the halyard away from the mast, while you check that it hasn't fouled the backstay, shrouds, or spreaders. If it's clear and free, make the halyard shackle fast to the head cringle.

Insert the battens. If the sail has the new, self-closing pockets, make sure the battens are fully inserted and pushed down in the pocket proper. If the pockets are the older type, with ties (nettles), lead the line through the eye in the batten ends and tie the lines with a secure *square* or reverse *surgeon's* knot (see p. 85). Very likely the battens for a given sail will be of two or three different sizes—short for top and bottom pockets, long ones in the middle. Be sure the battens fit the pockets they're in, and have at least one spare of each size aboard. Wood battens may be varnished, and it doesn't hurt to write the batten size right on the wood—"12 x 1½"—before varnishing.

While slowly raising the sail, slip the luff slides onto the track in the proper order, in the same way you did with the foot slides. Hoist the sail far enough to be sure that every slide has been attached, and is facing the right way, then lower and furl it loosely (see p. 39) until the jib is bent. (Obviously, feeding a sail's roped edge into a groove is much simpler—so much so that there's really no need to describe it.)

Unlike the mainsail, the jib can usually be bent on right out of the bag—if it's been stowed so the tack cringle is immediately accessible. Make the cringle fast to the tack fitting (81), and then attach the snaps in order, beginning with the first one up from the tack. If there are no twists in the luff, all the snaps will face the same way on the stay once they're attached.

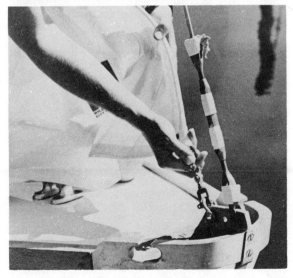

81

Insert the jib battens, if any, and attach the jib sheets to the clew cringle. Some sailors splice the sheets to the cringle, which makes for a most secure attachment. But it also means that you have to have a separate pair of sheets for each jib. In order to avoid this expense and complication, most skippers tie or snap the sheets to the jib clew.

Check jib and main sheets once again, to make sure they can run free when the sails are hoisted. If the boat is facing more or less into the wind, you can now raise the sails to check their fit and tension.

First hoist the main as high as it will go without jamming the halyard splice in the masthead sheave, or hoist it to the height of peak mark used in many racing classes (mark the halyard to indicate the proper point, down at your end, in either case). This should lift the boom out of its crotch so it can swing free. If the boat has a fixed—non-sliding gooseneck, the crew will have to sweat up the sail to make sure all slack is out of the halyard, before cleating it. The main halyard cleat is usually on the starboard side, the jib cleat to port; thus even a stranger aboard will know which is which.

With masts that have a sliding gooseneck, slack along the luff is removed by cleating the halyard with the sail hoisted, and pulling on the boom downhaul, at the base of the gooseneck (see illustration, p. 9). This fitting is usually a power-of-two block, and is quite sufficient to tighten the luff

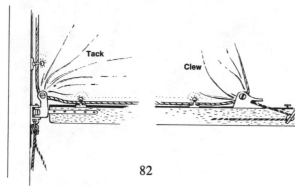

82

without imposing unnecessary strain.

Back off and take a look at the sail. If possible, hold the boat in position (at a

pier or float, say) and take in the mainsheet until the sail fills. While Dacron sails may have more wrinkles than well-fitting cotton canvas ones, the wrinkles to beware of are the ones—like those in the illustrations (82)—that show improper tension.

If the sails set properly, the halyard can be coiled so that it doesn't flap about, but so that it can be let run if the sail has to come down in a hurry. If the halyard cleats are high enough off the deck, you can suspend the coiled halyard from the cleat, as shown (83). If there's a coaming to keep the halyard end from slipping over the side, it can be left in a loose, capsized coil at the foot of the mast. Or it can be tucked between halyard and mast, above the cleat.

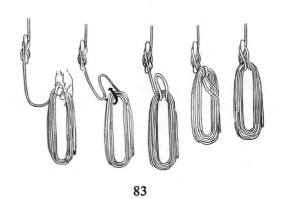

83

Since it's always a good idea—when possible—to practice a maneuver in peace and quiet before trying it under stress, practice lowering the mainsail right at the dock or mooring. Cast loose the halyard coil, checking again that it'll run free. Make sure the bitter end is fast or held by someone: otherwise, it'll almost certainly escape up the mast, and, very likely, right through the sheave. (If a halyard does unreeve itself this way, the illustrations (84 & 85) suggest two ways to get it back.)

Set up the boom crotch, if you removed it, and slack off the halyard until the boom is in its slot. Now lower the sail smartly, flaking it down (86) over the boom. If the sail jams part way down, a sharp tug on the halyard should free the slide.

With the sail down, cleat the bitter end of the halyard and unshackle the other

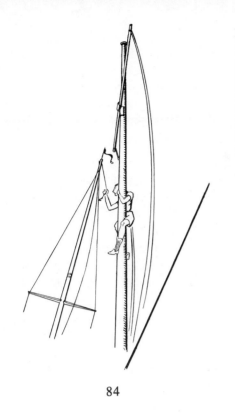

84

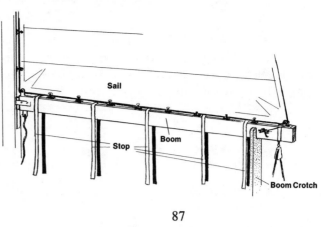

87

being lowered for a couple of hours, it's much easier simply to furl it on the boom.

Like this:

Slip four or five stops (gaskets) (87) between the foot of the sail and boom (it's easier if you do it before lowering the sail). With sail down and flaked, extend it as far aft along the boom as you can, flake by flake, to remove wrinkles. Pull the bottom flake—the largest—to one

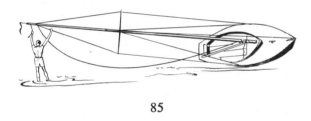

85

end from the head cringle, making it fast in a convenient spot. Remove the battens and put them someplace where they won't be stepped on or kicked overboard.

Most small boat sailors remove and bag the sail after each trip, but if a sail's only

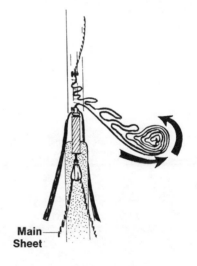

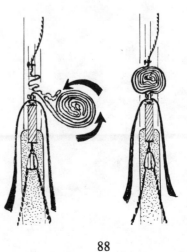

88

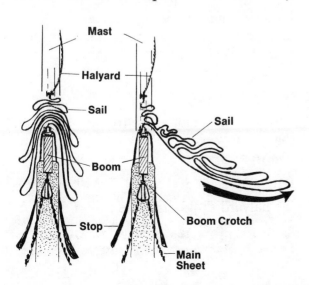

86

side, making a fold that'll hold the rest of the sail (88). Roll it toward the boom, tightly and evenly, so that the roll finishes lying atop the boom in a smooth furl.

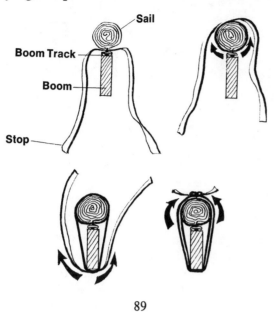

89

Needless to say, this is a lot easier for two people than one.

While holding the roll in place, bring the stops over the roll, down under the boom, and up again, to be tied at the top of the boom (89) in a square or slip knot (see p. 85).

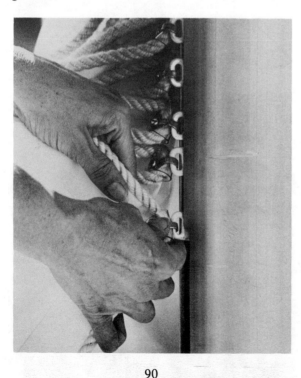

90

Shock cord stops are, of course, a great deal simpler. The only precaution, for beginner and old salt alike, is to make certain the toggle is securely in the loop before letting go: if it hasn't caught securely, the elastic shock cord will snap itself over the side, quick as thought.

But suppose we're taking the sail home. Skip back to the previous page, where we had the sail flaked out on the boom, battens removed, and halyard detached. Slack the outhaul, release the mainsail tack from the gooseneck fitting, and unshackle the clew. Open the gate at the bottom of the mast track and slip the slides off, or slip the slugs out of an internal track (90). Now stuff the mainsail head into the bag, and as much more of the sail as you can. When you've used up all the slack, slide the foot off the boom and stuff the rest of the sail into the bag. Trying to fold a sail neatly in a small boat's cockpit is not easy; it's far better to find a clear stretch of lawn or a clean dock and do it there.

Begin by stretching the sail out. Now fold it, accordion fashion, in loose flakes, parallel to the foot. The fewer creases, the better. Remember to put it into the bag so you have the clew cringle right to hand next time.

Hoisting the jib is a little different. Take up the jib halyard as taut as you can, and then cleat it. On some medium-sized daysailers, there's a downhaul arrangement at the jib tack, but on most, the sail must simply be sweated up. As you did with the main, take in a sheet until the sail fills. The luff should be straight, and so should the stay it's snapped to. If the jib luff is scalloped, the luff isn't under sufficient tension: quite often, this deficiency doesn't show until the boat's under way, with the sail pulling hard—at which point adjustment is a real pain in the neck. As a general rule, the luff should be as taut as you can make it—but not as taut as the forestay, so when that stay begins to slacken, you know you've overdone it.

Now check the lead of the jib sheets from clew to deck fairlead.* The consensus to-

*(fairlead) *A piece of hardware through which a line passes, a* fairlead *guides the line in the required direction, while chafing it as little as possible.*

91

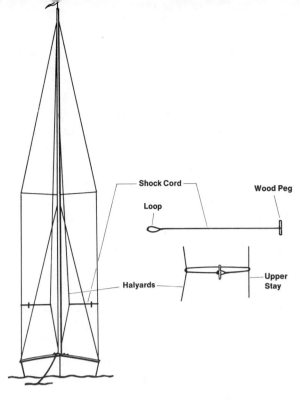

Shock Cord
Loop
Wood Peg
Halyards
Upper Stay

92

day seems to be that the jib sheet should lead just a bit below an extension of the miter seam (91). This is an approximation, however; final adjustment must be done while sailing, by noting that the foot and head of the sail should luff simultaneously when the boat is slowly brought into the wind.

On both main and working jib, the pull along the luff must be straight, which means that head and tack fittings shouldn't twist the sail out of line by being too big or too small.

Now drop the jib by uncleating the halyard and easing it out smoothly, while guiding the sail down with your free hand. It may be necessary to pull the last couple of feet of sail down the stay, in which case pull it by the reinforced luff, *not* the leech.

You can furl the jib, but since it usually doesn't have a boom, the furl will be less neat and the sail will rest on the deck, picking up dirt. It's also dangerous: Dacron is not as slippery as ice—not quite, but nearly.

Before bagging the jib, remove the battens: even short, stubby wood battens can damage the sail or set into a permanent bend.

Dacron sails should be stowed dry when possible. If it's not too windy, a few minutes' luffing at anchor will shake the water off them. If you have to stow them wet, don't pack them into an airless space: it's an invitation to disfiguring mildew.

Before leaving the boat, make the main halyard shackle fast to the outhaul (assuming you're not going to unstep the mast), and the jib halyard shackle fast to the jib tack fitting. Take the slack out of

the halyards and fasten them away from the mast with shock cord stops (92): there's nothing more maddening in an anchorage than the ceaseless *tunk-tunk-tunk* of slapping halyards left by thoughtless sailors.

Coil the halyards and place them, if you can, out of the sun—direct sunlight over a long period makes Dacron deteriorate, and in many of today's harbors, airborne grit will work into the fibers of exposed lines, weakening and dirtying them.

If you don't unship the rudder, lash the tiller amidships (93); pull up and secure the centerboard, and you're ready to go ashore.

93

13: Leaving Mooring or Pier

The novice sailor should, if he can arrange it, learn how to handle a boat on the various points of sailing and how to jibe and come about *before* he undertakes close-quarters handling in and around harbors and anchorages. Once you've got tacking and jibing down well, you're ready for the more advanced aspects, beginning with leaving the mooring.

The sails are up, we'll say, and luffing gently, the sheets ready to be trimmed as required, the boat and crew set to go. Before committing the boat to this or any maneuver, take time to plan ahead: look around and note the positions of other boats, anchored and under way; calculate not only your first move, but two or three beyond that; and always allow yourself an escape hatch when you can—some alternate plan if the maneuver doesn't work.

You know your boat, when first cast loose, won't be moving, and she won't handle smartly until she picks up speed, so don't plot any tricky courses right at the start. Lower the boat's centerboard for maneuverability.

Considering only wind for the moment, our boat sets off in standard fashion by drop-

95

ping the mooring (94). As the boat gathers sternway, follow one of the procedures described on p. 25 for getting out of irons. Let's say you extend the jib clew, backing that sail (95). The boat swings off the wind, with the mainsail luffing, and once the

94

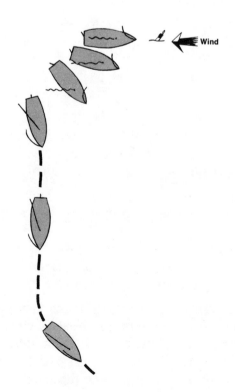

96

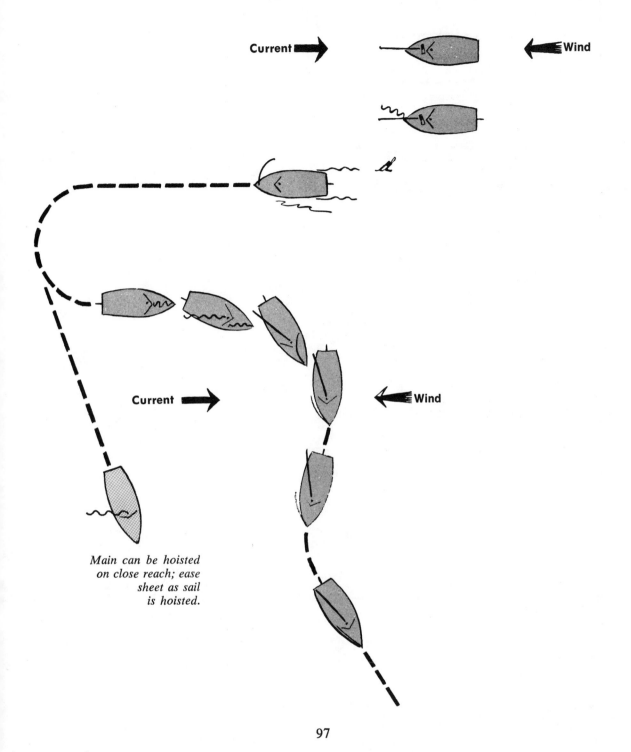

Current →   ← Wind

← Wind

Current →   ← Wind

*Main can be hoisted
on close reach; ease
sheet as sail
is hoisted.*

97

breeze is abeam, you trim sails and put the boat on her course (96).

In some circumstances, wind and current may be from opposite directions, with the current the stronger force. In this situation, bend on the mainsail ready to raise, but hoist only the jib and cleat its halyard. Cast off the mooring, trim the jib, and run down under jib alone until the boat is clear of obstructions. Now bring her up into the wind, and, as she rounds up, hoist mainsail smartly, while it luffs (97). Some sea room

for drifting must be allowed here, but once the main halyard is secured, you're ready to back the jib and sail away.

Leaving a pier is basically the same as dropping a mooring, except that the skipper should let his boat's sternway carry her well away from shore, to obtain clear air and sufficient maneuvering room.

If a boat is bow on to a pier, with other craft on both sides, all head to wind, then the departing boat should be walked back

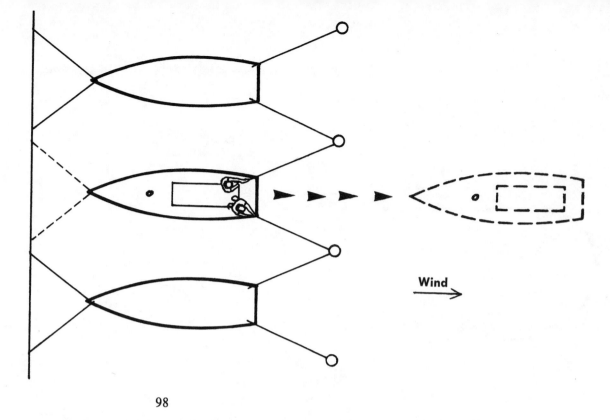

98

until she is completely free of her neighbors (98).

Once under way, check the set of all sails and make adjustments immediately: not only do badly-setting sails mark a landlubber, they also mean poor performance.

If you're sailing away from a beach, one crew member should stand on the beach at the bow (99), until the boat is ready to sail away. Unless shallows extend well out from shore, you'll have to sail either away from land or parallel to it, no matter what the wind's doing. The crew member at the bow will have to be quite agile to help push the boat off and get aboard just as the sails fill and the boat gains way. (Of course the ideal arrangement in this situation is to recruit a volunteer from shore to hold the bow.)

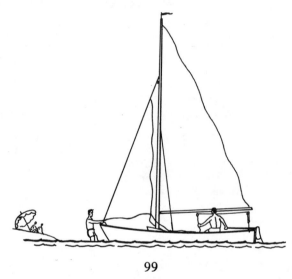

99

14: Picking Up a Mooring, Docking and Landing

Approaching and picking up the mooring at the end of a day's sail can be the satisfying capstone to your voyage, or a complete disaster. Which it's to be depends on the skipper. The idea is simple enough: bring the boat up into the wind, in irons, so that the forward momentum dies just as the buoy comes within the crew's grasp (100).

As always, planning is the key. Consider in advance what to do if the boat undershoots the mooring, or glides past it: on which side will you have to back the jib to fall off safely without fouling other boats (101)?

Here's the textbook situation, which will often happen in real life, too.

2. Drop, unsnap, and bag the jib (102). If there isn't time to do all three, furl the jib with a stop or two and lay it to one side of the deck, as far from the mooring cleat as possible. If the boat is unhandy under main alone (likely, if the mast is stepped well aft), then you'll simply have to leave the jib up and work around it.

100

1. Approaching the mooring close-hauled, drop the board all the way down for maneuverability.

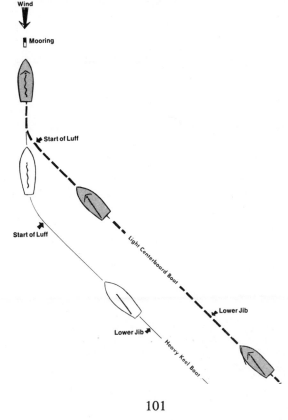

101

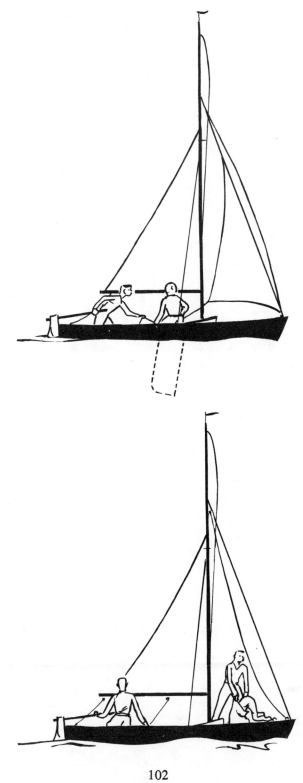

102

3. Judging the proper distance from the mooring, shoot up into the wind and have your crew pick up the mooring pendant. The "proper distance" will, of course, vary not only with the individual boat, but also with different wind and sea conditions. For many small centerboard boats under main alone, one or two boat lengths is plenty for light airs; and perhaps three in strong breezes. A heavy keel type, as shown, will often need more room. Practice with a dummy mooring is the only way to build up the necessary experience.

4. Having made fast the mooring pennant, drop and furl the mainsail (103). So much for the ideal situation. In crowded harbors —and most of them are jammed these days —a straight beat up to the mooring may not be possible. It may be necessary to run down past the buoy, then round up swiftly

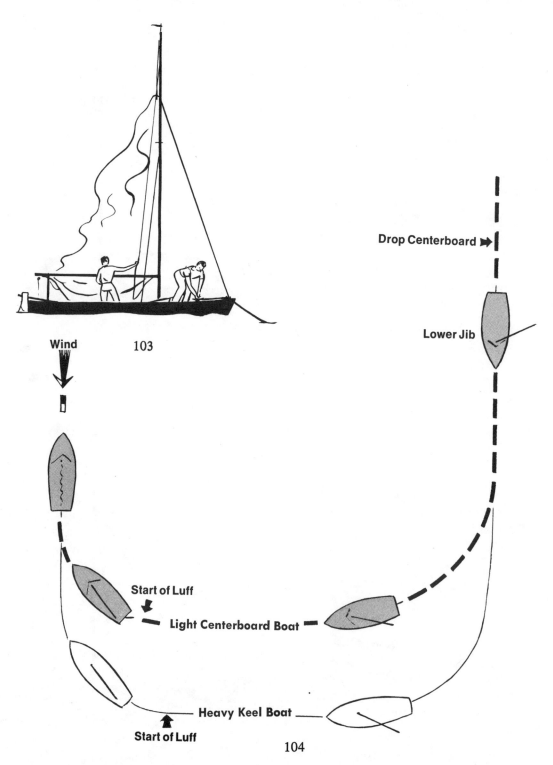

Wind   103

Drop Centerboard

Lower Jib

Start of Luff

Light Centerboard Boat

Heavy Keel Boat

Start of Luff

104

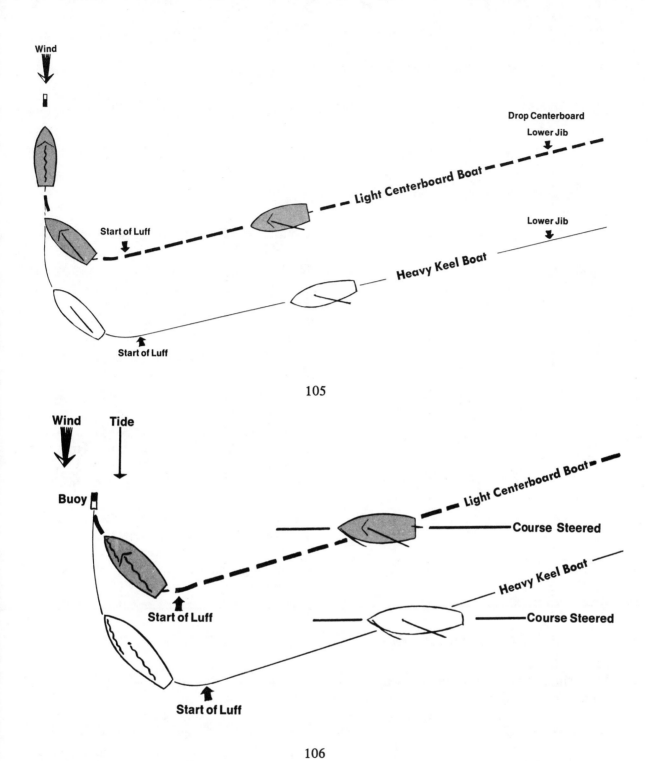

Wind

Drop Centerboard
Lower Jib

Light Centerboard Boat

Start of Luff

Lower Jib

Heavy Keel Boat

Start of Luff

105

Wind   Tide

Buoy

Light Centerboard Boat

Course Steered

Start of Luff

Heavy Keel Boat

Course Steered

Start of Luff

106

(104). Or the only clear path into the anchorage may be a reach (105).

Whenever wind and current act with considerable force, the best practice is to leave all sail set for maximum manueverability, and come in on a reach (106). In this case, especially, it is well to plan on an alternate course of action in case you miss the buoy the first time.

Then there will be times when wind and current are opposed, with the current the stronger (107). In this case the safest practice is to drift upwind, in irons. An alternative is to sail downwind with just enough jib to overcome the current.

Approaching a pier is basically the same as shooting for a mooring, except that the results of an overshoot can be very serious. While an error on the side of too much speed is perhaps better when shooting for a mooring, quite the opposite is true when heading for a pier.

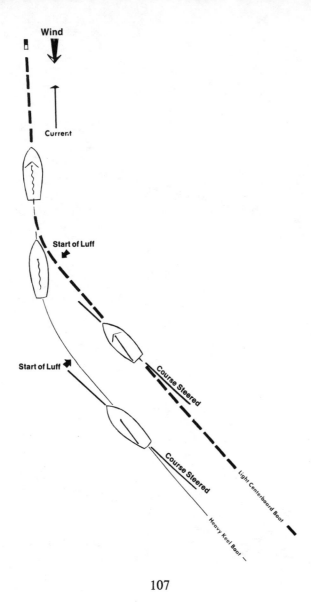

107

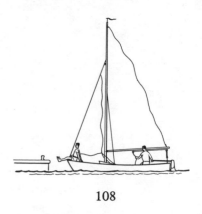

108

Coming in bows on, the crew should sit—never stand—on the foredeck, prepared to fend off with his shod feet (108). When there's a choice, it's better to aim for a low float than a high dock: aside from ease of disembarking, a float will have far less effect on wind force and direction. Never count on the padding that edges many floats and docks: there may be hidden nail-heads waiting to scar the topsides.

As mentioned earlier, approaches to the beach should be made slowly and under full control, rounding up offshore. The crew member assigned to hold the bow while sails are lowered should never leap into the water until he knows, first, how deep it is, and second, what's on the bottom. Unless the water's completely clear over a white sand bottom, discretion calls for leaving one's deck shoes on when wading off beaches today.

15: Anchoring and Moorings

Most small boat ground tackle is light and simple, quite different from that found on deep-water crusiers. But every boat—except perhaps cockpitless boards and catamarans—should carry a reliable anchor and an anchor rode strong enough and long enough for the waters she frequents. Ten times the high-water depth in a boat's customary harbor is a good yardstick. Between the anchor and the rode you should have from 3 feet to 12 feet of the appropriate size chain. Small dinghies need only 3 feet of light chain. Cruising boats will need more. Chain keeps the rode low to maximize the anchor's holding power.

As for the type of anchor, that's a matter for local judgment. A newcomer will do

well to check with knowledgeable local skippers and see what they recommend. In the absence of that kind of information, here is a brief rundown of small boat anchors in wide use, with the salient characteristics of each.

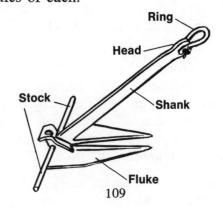

109

1. Danforth (109): lightweight, with high holding power in bottoms that allow the big, sharp flukes to bite. Stows flat or in patent holder. Not too good in rocks or very heavy kelp, where it may skip along the bottom or get choked with weed.

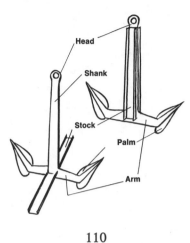

110

2. Northill (110): another lightweight with good holding power in a wide assortment of conditions. The Northill's stock folds, but it will not stow as flat as a Danforth.

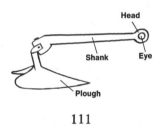

111

3. Plow (111): a favorite of cruising skippers. It's very difficult to stow easily, except under a bowsprit. Good holding power in a wide range of bottom conditions, except rocks.

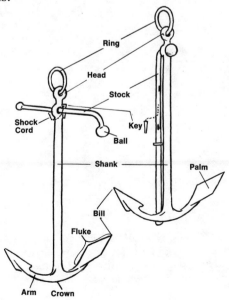

112

4. Yachtsman's (112): the traditional folding anchor. Flukes may be small and sharp, for hard sand, or wide and flat, for mud. This anchor doesn't hold as strongly as a lightweight anchor of similar weight in most conditions, but it's more effective for rocky bottoms.

113

5. Folding grapnel (113): the four-prong grapnel folds and stows easily, and will hold very well in rocky conditions, though not so well in others.

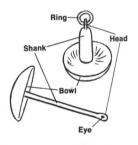

114

6. Mushroom (114): lines won't snag on this one, but it requires some time to dig its way into the bottom. The larger sizes are often used for permanent moorings, the smaller ones by fishermen for short stops.

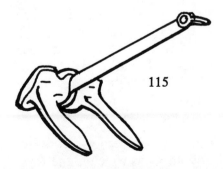

115

7. Stockless or Navy (115): not much good for yachtsmen generally or especially for sailors, where weight in the boat is important.

Ideally a good anchorage should offer at least two things: secure holding ground in which to set the anchor, and protection from prevailing winds and seas. Your chart* will show depth of water and composition of the bottom; this, along with tide and current information, should be known before anchoring.

coiled loosely and ready to run. Make sure the rode's bitter end is made fast: lines and anchors are expensive.

Bring the boat up into the wind, in the desired spot, just as in approaching a mooring: the difference is that this time you'll be dropping your anchor, not picking it up. The skipper should know more or less how

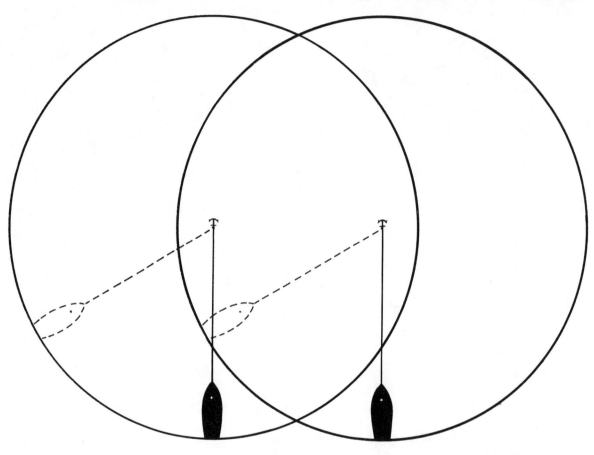

116

When there's a choice, the wise skipper anchors among boats like his own in size and type, and at a minimum of three to four boat lengths from the nearest other vessel. Similar boats react to wind and current in similar ways—they'll be wind- or tide-ridden together, and in the same direction. If possible, a skipper should find out how much scope (116) his neighbors are riding to, so that the swinging circles of nearby boats won't impinge on each other.

Approaching the anchorage, lower the jib, unsnap and stow it, so as to leave the foredeck free. Larger boats often carry an anchor in chocks on deck (117), but this is impractical for most daysailers. The anchor should be made fast to its rode, the line

117

*(chart) *A chart is simply a nautical map—a stylized picture of a portion of the earth, drawn to a given scale. Where maps emphasize land features, charts concentrate on those on and under the water.*

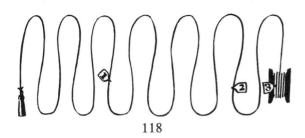

118

119

—between five and ten times the depth, depending on weather conditions and the expected length of one's stay. A scope of seven to one (line to depth) is a good compromise in reasonably sheltered waters (120).

122

deep the water is, but it's wise to check anyway. Most small boats don't carry a sounding line (118), but it's easy to mark the anchor rode itself, with tape or the patent plastic markers sold by marine suppliers (119).

Lower the anchor carefully over the side, once the boat is dead in the water. When you feel it touch bottom, check the depth and stop feeding line until the boat gathers sternway, then pay out as much as required

Before making the rode fast to the bow cleat, give a sharp tug on the line to make sure the anchor is holding (121). Boats with auxiliary power often put the engine briefly into reverse to set the hook. And if you're planning to stay at anchor for more than an hour or so, it's a good idea to rig chafing gear (122) at those points where the line can rub against any surface. Tape makes an adequate temporary guard,

120

121

but better are split lengths of rubber tubing or hose prepared for the purpose.

A good skipper soon develops an eye for landmarks, so he can observe if the boat is holding her position or not. If she seems to be moving, it's generally possible to feel the anchor dragging by holding the rode, outboard of the bow chocks, between one's fingers.

Rocky anchorages may result in a fouled anchor—one that gets hooked under a rock too large to move. The answer is a buoyed trip line: tie a piece of light line—¼″ braided nylon's a perfect size—to the crown of the anchor before lowering it, and feed this line over the side at the same pace as the rode itself, but separately, to avoid tangles. The light line must be at least as long as the maximum depth of water to be

124

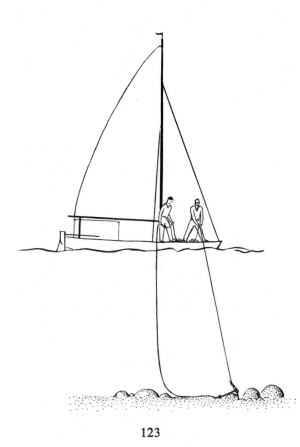

123

expected, with a few feet left over. At its end, make fast a small buoy, such as a sealed plastic detergent bottle with molded-in handle.

Then, if the anchor should foul, you can simply haul it out backwards (123 & 124) with the trip line.

If an anchor fouls with no trip line rigged, a swimmer can sometimes go down and free it, and as a last resort, the skipper can try to sail it out. Let out enough rode so the boat can maneuver, but no more. Hoist the mainsail and then sail in very tight circles

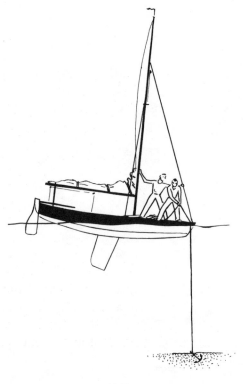

125

126

around the anchor, keeping as much tension on the anchor rode as possible.

An anchor set deep into sticky mud may refuse to come up without being fouled at all. It can, however, be levered up, as shown in the illustrations: first, move all the crew as far forward as possible and take in on the rode till it's straight up and down, and as taut as you can get it (125). Now move all hands aft, and as the bow lifts, it may bring the anchor up with it (126). More effective action can be obtained on a rising tide.

Moorings

Most clubs and marinas set out and maintain their own moorings, renting them to yachtsmen. It's still a good idea to know what makes up a reliable mooring rig. For daysailers in the 16-20 foot range—boats a little too hefty for easy trailer launching —the illustrated mooring should work adequately (127). In sheltered waters, a 75-lb. mushroom anchor is a good size, while a somewhat heavier mushroom, about 125-lb., is required for exposed anchorages. The chain should be about ½″ in diameter and the mooring line not less than ½″ nylon, well served with chafing gear. In northern waters, the pickup buoy should be removed in winter and—if you can manage it—so should the anchor and chain. In areas where boating continues the year around, the mooring should be carefully inspected by a Scuba diver at least annually, with special attention paid to the shackle pins at anchor and buoy. These pins should be wired, to prevent their backing off by themselves.

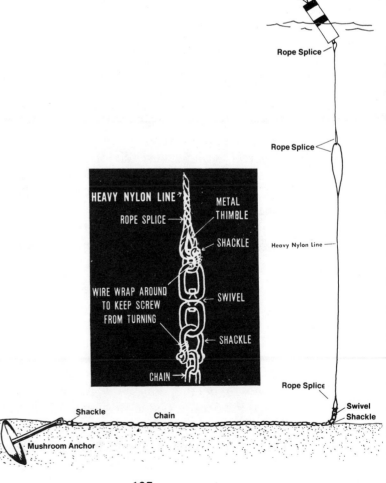

127

16: Tuning, Balance and Trim

Earlier in this book, we considered the elementary tuning involved in seting up a small sailboat's mast and rigging. Chances are that after the boat's been under way for a few hours, on several points of sailing, the skipper will discover that additional tuning is necessary. Bear in mind the most important thing to strive for in most boats is a straight mast at all times.

With the boat moving, turn the helm over to a crew member and sight up the forward side of the mast. (We're assuming a boat with one set of uppers and one of lowers.) If the masthead bows to windward (128) on either tack, the lower shrouds on the windward side are too slack, or the uppers are too tight, or both.

If the masthead bows to leeward, then the upper shroud on the windward side is probably too slack, or the lowers too tight.

Next, sight up the side of the mast. If the masthead bows forward, especially when the boat is close-hauled (129), it means the backstay is probably too slack. If it bows aft, the backstay may well be too taut. This only holds true, of course, for boats whose masts aren't supposed to bend. There's a whole new school of boats with so-called *bendy* masts, the bend in them being applied by the backstay or the mainsheet pulling along the leech. Bendy masts only bend aft at the top, and they are bent when the boat is under way close-hauled.

Lee and Weather Helm

A boat's *balance* has to do with how well she will hold a course by herself. When under way on a reach, in a light wind with sails properly trimmed, only a very light touch on the tiller should be necessary to maintain a straight course. If the boat has a tendency to round up into the wind, so

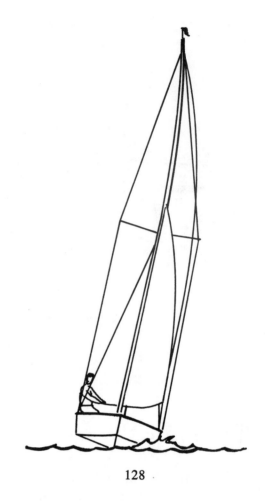

128

129

that you have to hold the tiller to windward or *weather* to maintain the heading, then your boat is said to carry a *weather helm*.

Conversely, if the boat tends to fall away to leeward under the same conditions, she has a *lee helm*.

The technical reasons for lee and weather helm are illustrated in the accompanying diagram (130). What's important to remember is that the constant corrective steering required in a badly balanced boat will slow her down greatly, so that it really pays to try for a well-balanced hull and rig.

From the point of view of safety, a slight amount of weather helm is desirable: if for some reason the tiller has to be abandoned temporarily, it's far better for the boat to round up slowly into the wind by herself, than for her to fall off into an uncontrolled jibe.

Weather helm may suddenly appear in a boat during strong winds, or when a boat is sharply heeled, but it should abate once the wind eases or the boat is righted. Corrections of lee or weather helm fall into two categories—temporary (131) and permanent (132)—and they're diagrammed below (133). (When applying corrections, remember that the heavier the boat, the more severe the correction that will be required.)

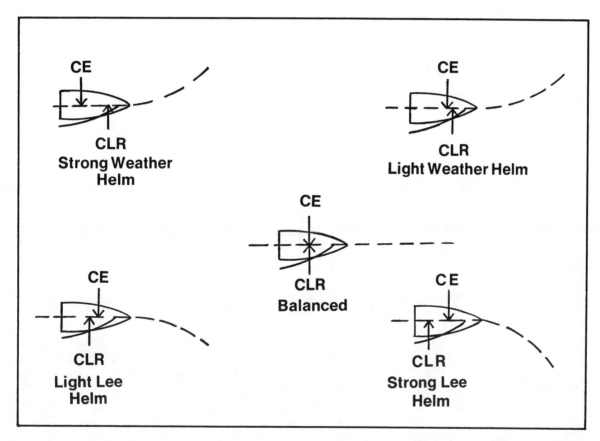

130

Diagrams above illustrate the principle involved when the CE (center of effort) shifts relative to the position of the CLR (center of lateral resistance). Naturally, there could never be such wide discrepancies between the two points in practice. For purposes of illustration, the differences have been greatly exaggerated. As CE shifts further aft, the stronger the weather helm. As CE moves forward, ahead of the CLR, we get lee helm. The center illustration shows a theoretically balanced condition.

TEMPORARY CORRECTIONS WHEN UNDER WAY

TO CORRECT WEATHER HELM

Sail the boat with less heel—By moving the crew as far to windward as possible or by keeping a flutter in the sail, thereby sailing the craft as close to its designed waterline as possible.

If pivoted, raise the centerboard—Until an effect is noticed on the helm.

Ease the main sheet—Thereby reducing side pressure on the mainsail.

Haul on the jib sheet—This increases side pressure on the sail, OR do both of the above.

TO CORRECT LEE HELM

On small boats with low aspect ratio rig, shift the crew forward—as far as needed; this lowers the bow, causing it to grip deeper in the water, and raises the stern. Speed may be affected adversely.

Sail the boat with more heel—This increases its waterline length and alters the immersed shape.

Shift the movable heavy weights forward—This causes the bow to dip.

Lower the centerboard—Until pressure on the tiller is reduced.

Haul in on the main sheet—This increases its side pressure.

Slack the jib sheet—This relieves side pressure on the sail, OR do both of the above.

131

PERMANENT CORRECTIVE MEASURES

Of the listings below any one or several in combination can be effective

TO CORRECT WEATHER HELM

Decrease the rake in the mast—Tip the mast forward to a more upright position, keeping the heel in the same position. Stays and shrouds must also be readjusted.

Step the mast forward—Entire mast moves forward. The stays and shrouds must also be readjusted.

Move the centerboard pin aft—This moves a pressure factor aft.

Move the jib stay forward—Allows for larger fore triangle and moves its center forward.

If jib is small, increase the size of the jib—This also allows for a larger fore triangle, particularly on those craft that cannot move the jibstay.

Decrease the size of the mainsail—This must be carefully done and done only after other methods have proved ineffective. A sailmaker should be consulted before any cutting is done.

Use a flatter mainsail—This decreases pressure as sail will not need to be trimmed as flat.

Soften a tight leech—Any leech that is not straight but has a tendency to curl to windward can cause quite an imbalance. This can be cured by resewing the seams near the leech.

TO CORRECT LEE HELM

Increase the rake of the mast—Keep heel of mast in same position—tip the mast aft—means readjusting of stays and shrouds.

Step the mast aft—Entire mast moves aft—stays and shrouds must also be readjusted.

Move the centerboard pin forward—Moves a pressure factor forward.

Move the jibstay aft—Reduces the pressure forward.

Reduce the size of the jib—This also reduces the pressures forward but means recutting the sail.

Increase the size of the mainsail—Means getting a new sail.

Use a fuller mainsail—One with more draft or belly; generally means resewing by a sailmaker.

132

Mainsail Trim

The principle behind proper trimming of the main might be abbreviated as *down and out*: ideally, the main boom should be pulled *down* to help flatten the sail, and it should be pulled from a point *out*ward of the centerline, for the most direct vertical force. The object is to have the sail maintain its airfoil shape at all elevations; this means that sheet traveller and vang must be adjusted so that the sail luffs simultaneously at all heights from head to foot when the boat is brought slowly into the wind.

When the boom lifts, the head of the sail sags off, and the effective sail area decreases (134). It is also possible to trim a sail too flat (especially in light airs), killing the proper airfoil curve: the most obvious symptom of over-trimming is a flatness along the inner line of the battens (135).

On a reach or run, the boom will tend to lift, and serious sailors counteract this by using a tackle called a *boom vang* or *kicking strap* (136). As the illustration suggests, it's simply a tackle running between the base of the mast and the under side of the boom, about one third of the way out-

Each of these two illustrations show how adverse helm can be cured when sailing. Sometimes only one change is necessary, other times a combination is needed before any improvement is noticed. (1) Adjusting sails, both jib and mainsail, or (2) raising or lowering the centerboard.

These three diagrams show (4) tipping the mast forward or aft, (5) moving the entire mast forward or aft, and (6) moving the jibstay forward or aft—are the easier of the permanent corrective methods for cure of adverse helm.

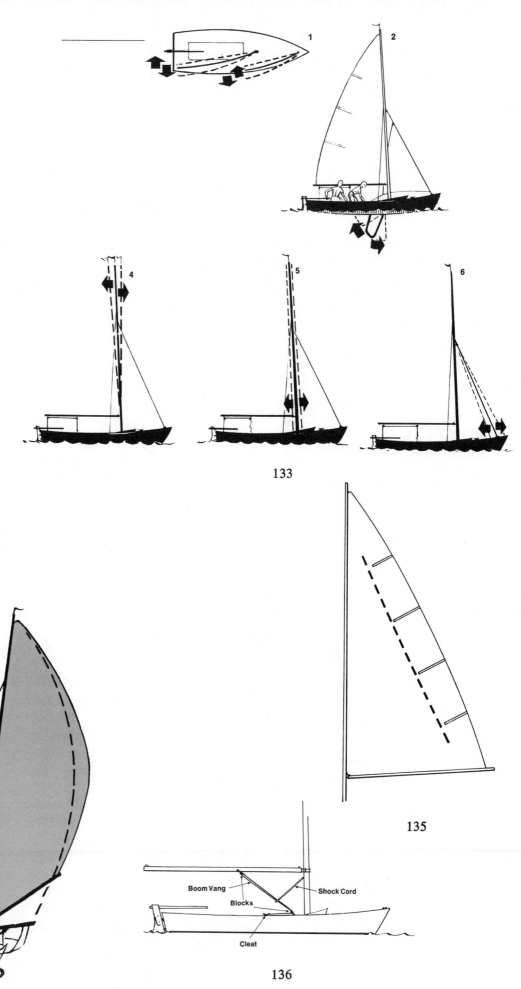

133

135

136

134

board. This vang is attached just before easing the sheet for a reach or run. A vang imposes great strains on the boom and the gooseneck, and it should be fitted by an expert if it didn't come as part of the boat's original gear.

Part IV: Light Weather Sails and Variant Rigs

Working sails are a boat's meat and potatoes: without them, she can't go. Light weather sails are more like dessert: they're not vital, but they add a great deal of pleasure.

Most light weather sails on a sloop are headsails, and the two most important are the genoa jib and the spinnaker, which we'll discuss in detail. Fad headsails come and go with such speed that it's really not possible in a book like this to deal with them adequately.

17: Genoa Jib, Reacher

Usually called a *jenny,* your boat's genoa jib is one of her most useful sails—more important, in many modern designs, than the working jib. The genoa began as a sail for use in very light airs; like the working jib, it's triangular, but it's usually longer on the luff and always longer on the foot (137):

Head

Tabling

Leech

Snaphooks

Reinforcing Patches

Luff

Wire Luff Rope

Clew

Clew Cringle Foot

Tack

137

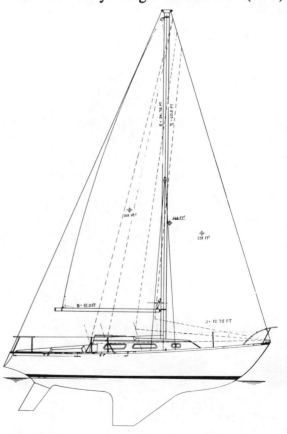

138

139

by definition, a genoa overlaps the mast. The leech may be a straight line or it may be cut in a reverse roach, making a long, inward curve from head to clew. Either way, it'll have no battens, since they'd take a ter-

rible beating against spars and shrouds when the boat came about.

Jennies have no set size, and many skippers carry an assortment, numbered from the largest (#1) to the smallest—usually a #5 (138). The maximum overlap is regulated by different racing organizations according to different formulas, and if you intend to race, your sails (like your boat) will have to conform to one rule or another.

While small boats usually stick with a single genoa, more and more skippers are turning to adjustable-size genoas (at some sacrifice to sail shape) which operate on a principle called *roller-furling*: as the illustration shows, the sail can be rolled about its luff wire, and as much of it exposed as desired. (139).

As you can easily imagine, the normal jib sheet leads won't suit the long-footed genoa, and often the regular jib sheets themselves will be too short. Most boats have a *track* installed along each gunwale, on which there rides a *slide* or *car* carrying the genoa lead block (140). In this way the genoa sheet lead can be varied for different sails or different points of sailing.

A genoa's pull, especially close-hauled, can be tremendous, and in boats over 16 feet or so, most skippers elect to install sheet

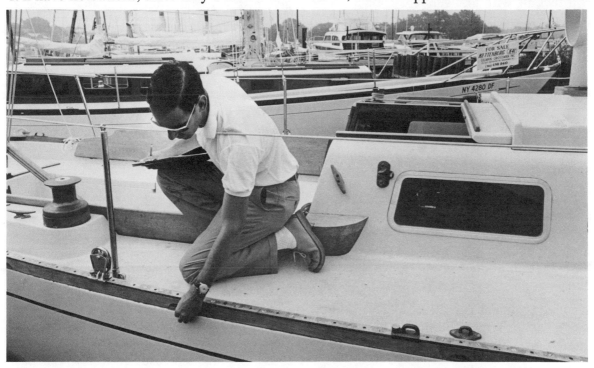

140

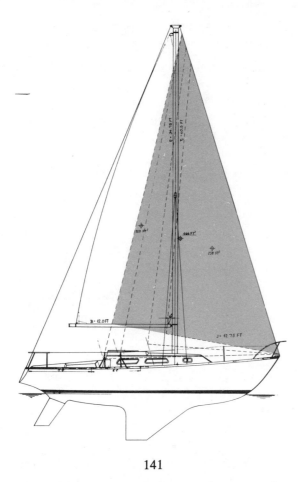

141

while a working jib's sheets may lead inside one or both shrouds.

When coming about with a jenny set, there's plenty of opportunity for the clew fittings to snag on projections, and for the sail itself to chafe badly. In larger boats, a crewman walks the genoa around shrouds and mast every time the boat tacks. In any case, a boat comes about more slowly with a jenny, and more momentum is thus required to keep from getting caught in irons.

As the wind pipes up, a whole new set of problems rises with it. The question of what sail to reduce, and how, is dealt with in detail in Chapter 21, but in general it's fair to say that many skippers prefer to reduce the mainsail area in gusty weather, as opposed to changing down to a smaller jib. Of course, roller furling makes reducing the jib's area the work of a moment.

Boats that carry several jennies make the #1 of very light fabric and the #2 of somewhat heavier material, but about the same size. Really serious racers may also have a sail that resembles the genoa, called a *reacher* (141). Where the genoa's great usefulness lies in increasing the efficiency of the jib-mainsail slot effect, the reacher (identifiable by its high-cut foot) is designed to provide the same sail area as a genoa, but higher up, and under reaching conditions. A reacher is sheeted well aft, often to the outer end of the main boom.

winches on the cockpit coamings, to give them some mechanical advantage in sheeting the genoa flat.

Too large a jenny may give a boat lee helm, and tacking with any genoa can be a problem: the overlapping foot must drag around shrouds and mast, and the sail must then be stretched past the other set of shrouds,

18: Spinnakers

By all odds the most beautiful, exacting, and maddening sail on today's boats is the spinnaker (142). While there are great differences among spinnaker designs, they all have certain fundamental points in common.

1. The spinnaker is a three-sided sail that's *set flying*—it's made fast only at its three corners, not along any of the sides.

2. Spinnakers are made of ultra-light fabric, generally nylon.

3. Most spinnakers are designed with a curved foot and two equal, curved sides.

Some spinnakers are bell-shaped, while others are nearly spherical. Many racing spinnakers, striving for that last square foot of area, have a flared skirt along the foot. Of the many possible patterns of spinnaker cloths, two of the most popular are shown (143). The bright colors so typical of today's spinnakers usually follow the pattern of the cloths.

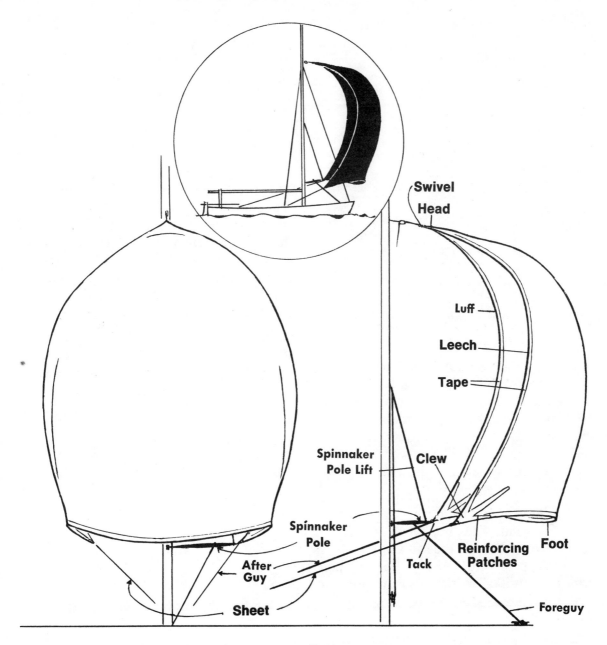

142

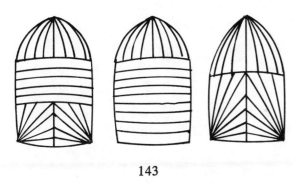

143

corners, which are interchangeable, are both called *clews* and the sides are both *leeches*—until the sail is set.

The spinnaker halyard runs through a block above and outside the jibstay, so the sail can set ahead of the stay. A chute's head fitting usually consists of a swivel, which allows the sail to untwist itself as it's being hoisted. Spinnakers are set when running or reaching.

The sail's windward edge (which now becomes its luff) is extended by a spinnaker pole, whose length equals the horizontal distance from the base of the mast to the forestay. Spinnaker poles generally have interchangeable ends, with a snap fitting at each (144). The inboard end is made fast to an

The nomenclature of spinnakers—also nicknamed *chutes* and *kites*—follows the same terms that apply to other sails, but uses them in a slightly different way. A spinnaker's top is still its *head,* and its lower edge its *foot,* but the two lower

eye on the forward side of the mast, sometimes fixed but usually adjustable along a vertical track. The pole's outboard end snaps around the forward end of the afterguy, but may, in light air, be snapped into the spinnaker's windward tack.

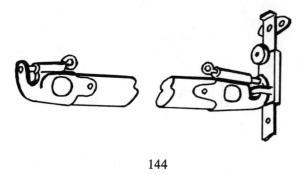

144

The sail is controlled by two primary lines, a *guy* to windward and *sheet*, leeward: the terms are temporary and exist to avoid confusion; the lines are identical, and change their names according to which tack the boat is on. The lower windward corner of the chute is now its *tack*.

When a spinnaker is trimmed properly, the pole is horizontal, and at right angles to the apparent wind. The guy, which is snapped to the same corner of the sail as the pole is, trims the pole fore and aft. Vertical pole trim is controlled by the mast eye and two additional lines, the *pole topping lift* and the *foreguy*.

The lift runs from the pole's balance point up through a block about halfway up the forward side of the mast, and then down to a convenient cleat, usually on the forward side of the mast near the deck, where it won't be used accidentally for something else. The topping lift exists to support the weight of the pole in light airs, when the spar's own weight would be enough to drag down the corner of the chute.

On most daysailers and small cruisers, there's a single foreguy, snapped to the outboard end of the pole and led back through either a block at the jib tack fitting or one farther aft on the foredeck to a point where it can be adjusted easily by the crew.

Hoisting the spinnaker isn't black magic, but it is a tricky operation that should be

practiced many times in calm waters, to get the hang of it. Let's assume that the boat's running with the wind over the starboard quarter, under main and genoa. The chute is in its bag, carefully folded so that all three corners are on top. The bag itself is attached to a deck fitting.

1. Make the clews fast to sheet and guy. These lines generally lead aft to blocks at the quarters, then back to cleats on the cockpit coamings. (They can, however, lead through the genoa sheet blocks set in their aftermost position.) Remember that the spinnaker sets outside of all the rigging, so sheet and guy must set outside the shrouds, and the guy goes *outside* the jibstay (145).

2. Make the pole fast to the spinnaker tack or guy and mast eye. On most small boats the guy will run free through the snap fit-

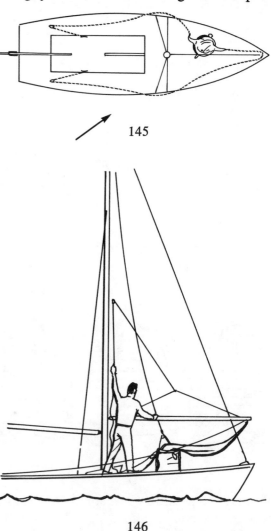

145

146

ting at the pole's outboard end. Raise the pole to its approximate correct position, using the topping lift and foreguy (146).

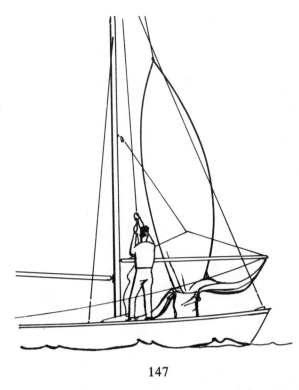

147

3. Snap on the spinnaker halyard, making sure it's not fouled. The halyard will now dangle loosely down the lee side of the jenny and under its foot.

4. You're ready to go. As the helmsman lets the boat fall off a little, till she's nearly on a dead run, hoist away smartly on the spinnaker halyard (147) and spread the sail with the sheet and guy.

5. The chute may have filled, but it's probably still hanging limp behind the jenny. Drop the genoa quickly, gathering it into a loose furl along the leeward rail. The spinnaker should now fill by itself, but if it doesn't, trim in the mainsheet a little (148). Once the boat gathers speed, you may trim the pole forward a bit, as the apparent wind moves toward the bow.

The difficult part, with a two-man crew, is handling the sheet and guy when the spinnaker is first hoisted, while at the same time steering, making fast the spinnaker halyard, and gathering the jenny. It's largely a question of timing, and the practice that leads to fast sail handling.

This is only one way of setting a kite. Many sailors hoist the sail from a *turtle,* a specially-designed sailbag with openings that help the sail emerge untwisted.

Others roll the sail (ashore on a lawn is the best place) and then stop it with turns of light thread. With the chute up, a simultaneous pull on the sheet and guy will cause

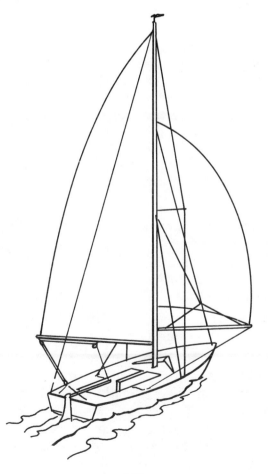

148

149

150

the lower stops to break; as the wind fills the chute, the remaining stops break in order.

151

On some points of sailing—notably beam reaches—it's possible to carry main, spinnaker, and jib at once (149), but as a general rule the jib will blanket the chute. Trying to fill the area beneath the spinnaker foot, some racing skippers set a *spinnaker staysail,* a light, nylon sail cut like a short-luffed genoa; it's set flying from a block partway up the mast, and tacked down to a cleat on deck (150).

Running, the spinnaker pole will extend out almost abeam (151), and as you head up onto a reach, the pole will have to be trimmed forward until, with the boat on a beam reach, it will be nearly touching the forestay—but don't let it rub against the wire, as both pole and stay will chafe badly.

Skippers with deep wallets carry a regular, full-cut chute and a very flat spinnaker, for reaching in winds slightly forward of the beam. For most of us, though, the genoa is not only more economical, but often more efficient, as so much of a spinnaker's force (when the boat is close reaching) is devoted merely to heeling and leeway.

down to where it can be unwound by hand, the best practice is to make for shore under main alone, or auxiliary power, and work on the problem in shelter. Running off and jibing the mainsail will often unwrap the spinnaker.

To avert spinnaker wraps, many owners use a net. One such device looks like the skeleton of a jib, hoisted on the forestay (152).

Lowering the spinnaker is just the reverse of hoisting it. First raise the jib or genoa, and if that doesn't blanket the spinnaker into submission, ease the pole forward and unsnap the tack fitting. As the chute col-

152

Because it's relatively difficult to control, a spinnaker is prone to more mishaps than other sails. One of the most serious is a *spinnaker wrap*, when the sail simply winds itself tightly around the headstay. A wrap is very hard to untangle, especially when under way. If the sail cannot be worked

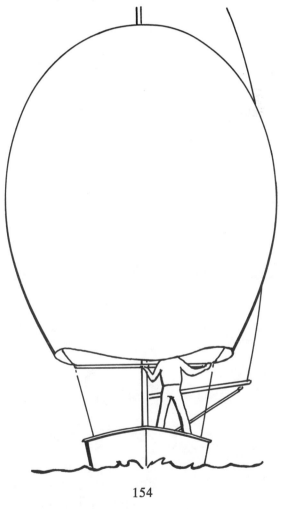

154

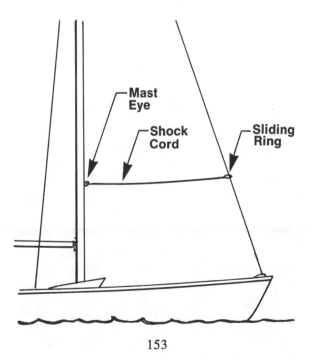

Mast Eye

Shock Cord

Sliding Ring

153

lapses, secure the clews and pull the sail down behind the mainsail. Don't let the spinnaker fall into the water, as it can be badly damaged and/or turn the boat out of control.

You cannot, obviously, come about with a

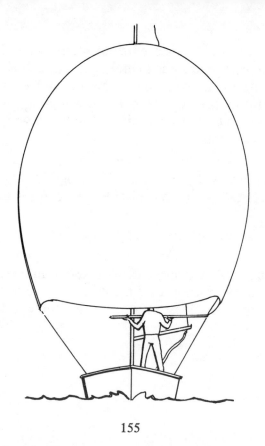

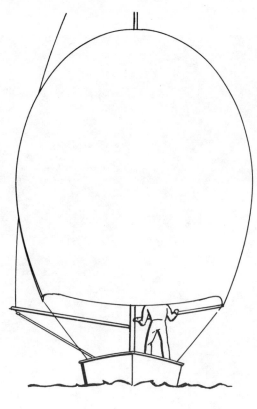

155

156

spinnaker set. But you can jibe, and it's not as terrifying as it might seem. Jibing the chute involves jibing the main as well, since the spinnaker pole must always be on the opposite side of the boat from the main boom. In a spinnaker jibe, the main is handled as it would be in any jibe.

1. As the skipper calls "Jibe-oh," and the boat begins to turn, the crew detaches the inboard end of the pole from the mast and clips it to the other clew of the chute (154).

2. The main boom comes over, and the crew detaches the pole snap (155) from

what had been the tack, and makes it fast to the mast eye (156). While this is in progress, another man trims the sheet and guy to keep the chute drawing. This means that easy jibing with a chute requires a crew of three. It can, however, be accomplished with two in calm weather—in which case the helmsman steers with the tiller between his knees and tends the sheet and guy with his hands.

3. There are more sophisticated methods used on larger boats, that will not be discussed here.

19: Variant Rigs

Over the centuries, hundreds of different sailing rigs have come and gone. The few that have achieved some permanence usually have some outstanding good qualities. In the following paragraphs, we will examine the ones most often seen in American waters today.

Yawl

When a boat gets about 45 feet in length, its main and jib become a problem for shorthanded crews. One solution is to break

up the total sail area into several smaller sails—though of course reducing the size of main and jib reduces their windward potential. The yawl is the racing man's compromise: it has a mainmast and fore-triangle* nearly as large as a sloop of equal size, plus a small mast aft called the *mizzen*. This after spar is stepped abaft the rudder post. The technical difference be-

* (fore-triangle) *The triangle formed by the main mast, jibstay, and a line drawn at deck level from the tack fitting to the base of the mast (or an extension of it).*

157

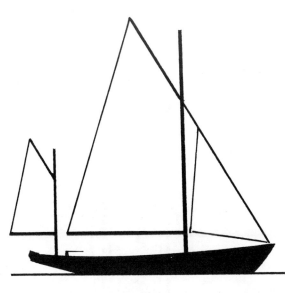

158

running sail, made of nylon. The mizzen staysail is set flying, sheeted to the end of the mizzen boom, and tacked down to a point on deck or cabin top to windward of the boat's centerline.

159

Ketch

The several working sails of a ketch are in more even proportion than those of a yawl, but she is less efficient to windward, because of her relatively small main and jib.

tween a yawl and a ketch is in where the mizzen is stepped: forward of the rudder post (ketch: 160, 161) or abaft it (yawl: 157, 158).

A yawl's mizzen sail is very small, providing little drive off the wind and less close-hauled. Under certain conditions, the mizzen provides needed balance against big jibs, and it allows the boat to shorten sail (see p. 77) easily. In theory, at least, a yawl can sail under jib and mizzen in heavy weather, but the resulting small sail area lacks power for driving into head seas.

The real advantage of the mizzen mast is that it allows the setting of a *mizzen staysail* (159), a light-weather reaching and

160

Ketch

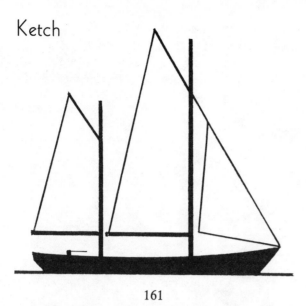

161

and the windage of her big mizzen. A ketch is the cruising man's twin-sticker, though a few ketches have done well enough in racing. A ketch mizzen is stepped forward of the rudder post—often right in the center of the cockpit—which can be both a nuisance and a safety factor, in that more of the necessary lines are right at the helmsman's hand. A ketch carries a big mizzen staysail, or sometimes two—a flat one and a full one.

Cutter

162

Another approach to reducing the area of individual sails is by splitting up the fore-triangle. A cutter's headsails are the jib,

set farther forward, and the forestaysail, often laced to a boom and self-tending.*

Cutters have good windward ability and can carry in light airs a huge genoa. Unfortunately, they often require *running backstays*†—releasable stays that attach to mast tangs at the same height as the staysail stay's tang, and leading aft. These are a considerable nuisance when tacking, which may be one reason that cutters have never achieved great popularity in the U.S.

The old definition of a cutter was a single-masted sailing vessel whose spar was stepped at least 40% of the distance aft from bow to stern, but this is hardly valid anymore, what with the great fore-triangles created by racing rules and modern materials. Most boats with double head rigs can be considered cutters.

Schooner

163

There are a number of possible rigs for schooners, which carry the mainmast aft, and a smaller *foremast* forward. The most

*(self-tending) *A self-tending headsail is one which does not have to be re-sheeted every time the boat comes about. Thus a boat with main and self-tending jib can be put about simply by putting the tiller over—no sheets need be handled at all.*
†(running backstays) *Only the windward running backstay is set up taut—usually by a lever on deck. The leeward one is slacked, to keep it from interfering with the mainsail and boom.*

Gaff
Schooner

164

MORGAN 22
LOA . . . 22' 6"
Beam . . . 8' 0"
Draft . . . 1' 10"
Sail Area . . . 238 sq ft

common arrangements for this typical American rig are the *staysail* (163) and the *gaff-rigged* (164). Schooners are relatively easy to work with a short-handed crew, because their biggest sail is well within the boat, but the mainmast often interferes with the accommodation, and the small fore-triangle makes them even worse to windward than ketches. Reaching, a good schooner sets a huge area of sail—jib, staysail, foresail, main topmast staysail (or gollywobbler, or fisherman), and mainsail—and can be very fast. Not usually seen in lengths under 40 feet.

ENSIGN
LOA . . . 22' 6"
Beam . . . 7'
Draft . . . 3'
Sail Area . . . 201 sq ft

CAPE DORY 10
LOA . . . 10' 6"
Beam . . . 4' 1"
Draft . . . 2'/5"
Sail Area . . . 68 sq ft

STAR
LOA . . . 22' 7½"
Beam . . . 5' 8"
Draft . . . 3' 4"
Sail Area . . . 285 sq ft

SUNFISH
LOA . . . 13' 10"
Beam . . . 4' ½"
Sail Area . . . 75 sq ft

SOLING
LOA . . . 26' 9"
Beam . . . 6' 3"
Draft . . . 4' 3"
Sail Area . . . 233 sq ft

PENGUIN
LOA . . . 11' 6"
Beam . . . 4' 6"
Draft . . . 4'/4"
Sail Area . . . 72 sq ft

HIGHLANDER
LOA . . . 20'
Beam . . . 6' 8"
Draft . . . 4' 10"/8"
Sail Area . . . 225 sq ft

DAY SAILER   LOA . . . 16' 9"
Beam . . . 6' 6"   Draft . . . 4'/8"
Sail Area . . . 145 sq ft

Part V: When the Going Gets Rough

Any sensible boatman avoids wind and sea conditions that will strain his boat or impose unnecessary risks, but sooner or later the time comes when heavy weather —or the threat of it—has to be faced. The novice sailor should make a special effort to steer clear of difficult conditions until he knows his boat and its capabilities as well as he knows his own skills. What follows is information to be read and digested in tranquility, to be used under stress; many of the procedures should be practiced on calm days until they're second nature. Then, when an emergency arises, you'll be ready to cope with it.

20: Wind and Weather

This isn't a weather book, and few small-boat sailors have the room aboard for the kind of complicated equipment required for accurate forecasting. The daysailing skipper is thus dependent upon the accuracy of shore forecasts and on his own observations. Every sailboat with a spray-proof locker should carry a portable radio, and taped to it a schedule of local *marine* weather broadcasts. Before leaving on even the shortest sail, get a weather forecast.

Learn the location of the nearest facility displaying small craft and storm warnings. If possible, make a visual check of its display before leaving port. A telephone call to the nearest U.S. Coast Guard station will provide an up-to-the-minute description of local wind and sea conditions.

But line squalls sometimes move so fast they outrace the forecasts. You should be able to recognize the appearance of the common storm cloud systems potential and actual.

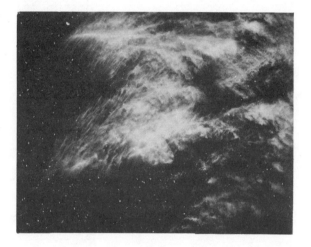

166

Cirrus (166)—a high altitude, feathery formation: when it thickens to produce the familiar *mackerel sky*, it means changing weather, often for the worse.

Cumulo-nimbus—the one to watch out for: these are the true thunderheads, capable of working into a savage storm in a half hour

165

Cumulus clouds (165)—rounded, puffy and bright: they usually indicate continued fair weather.

167

or so. In late summer, keep an eye on the puffy cumulus clouds, especially where sea and land meet: as the clouds heighten and darken, they are becoming more dangerous. Once the distinctive anvil shape (167) appears, a wise skipper will head for shore.

A reminder: sudden, sharp storms are generally over fairly soon; a storm that takes a long time in arriving will usually be around for a while, too.

Many years ago, Admiral Beaufort of the British Navy devised a scale that related sea conditions to wind speeds, in terms the average man could recognize. Below is a somewhat modified version for small craft.

Force	Speed (knots)	At sea	On land
0	0-1	flat calm	smoke rises vertically
1	1-3	boat under full sail has bare steerageway	smoke drifts slightly
2	4-6	wind fills small boat sails	leaves rustle, breeze felt on face
3	7-10	small boats heel and can plane (if so designed)	leaves in constant motion; small flags extended
4	11-16	small boats shorten sail; whitecaps form	small branches move; dust and paper blow
5	17-21	small boats seek shelter; large boats shorten sail	small trees sway
6	22-27	Larger boats shorten sail further.	umbrellas turn inside out
7 and above	28-plus	small craft should be in harbor	large trees move

21: Reefing

As the wind gets stronger and the boat heels more sharply, hiking out will not be enough, and other corrective measures are necessary. The first step in coping with heavy weather—aside from seeking shelter —is shortening sail. There are two ways of doing it: either by removing one or the other of the sails (see Chapter 22) or by reducing the area of one or both.

Decreasing a sail's area is called *reefing,* and the method used varies with the sail being reefed and the gear used to do it. In an earlier chapter, we dealt briefly with jib roller-furling gear, the most often seen method of reefing a jib. Mainsails can be reefed by the traditional *reef point* system, or by *roller reefing.*

Point reefing requires a row of grometted eyes across the sail, parallel to its foot and about the level of the lowest battens (168). Fixed in each eye is a short piece of light line, extending equally on both sides of the sail. At the leech and luff are slightly larger eyes, without lines, called the *leech reef cringle* and *tack reef cringle.* Two short lengths of line four to six feet long are

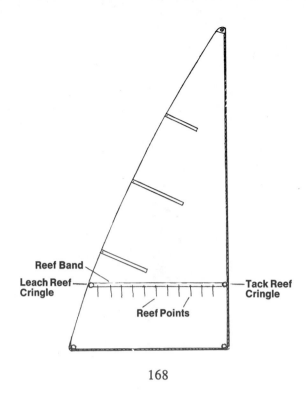

Reef Band
Leach Reef Cringle
Reef Points
Tack Reef Cringle

168

2. Put the boom crotch in place, lower the mainsail all the way, gathering it in as it comes down and shoving as much of it as possible down into the cockpit, to keep it from catching the wind (170). Haul the mainsheet in tight, to keep the boom from jumping out of the crotch.

3. Taking the two loose reefing lines mentioned above, use one to lash the tack reef cringle to the boom and forward to the gooseneck, to hold the cringle both down and forward (but be careful to avoid lashing it so that it interferes with the swing of the gooseneck); pull the leech cringle out along the boom, then lash it to the boom *and* to the outhaul with the second reefing line (171). The reef points should now be in a straight line along the top of the boom.

stowed in an accessible place for use in reefing.

While it's easier and safer to reef at the mooring, before setting out, much the same method is used to reef under way, and is more essential to know.

1. Head up into the wind, drop and furl the jib (169).

169

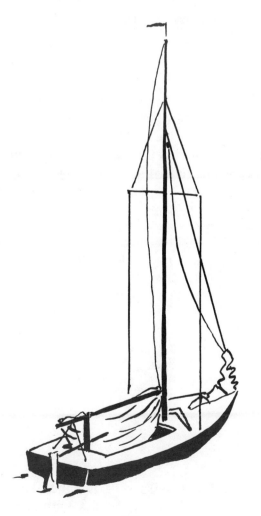

170

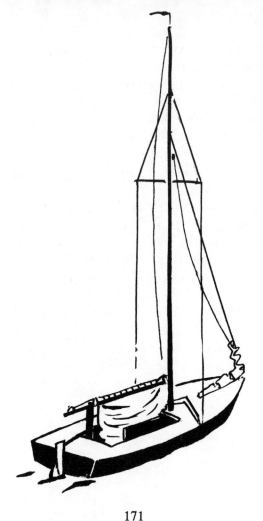

171

Reef Point

173

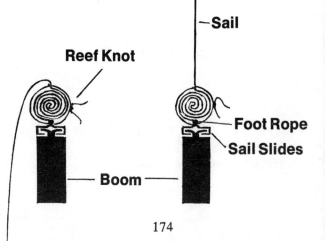

174

4. Removing the lower batten if necessary, take the flake of excess sail and roll it into a tight sausage (173).

5. To tie the reef in place with the paired reef points, lead the points down between the bolt rope and the boom (*not* under the boom) and tie each pair in a square or reef knot (see p. 85) (174). All the knots should be tight and in an even line, to put an equal strain all along the foot of the sail. The knots should, in addition, all be on the same side of the sail.

6. You're ready to sail away; assuming the bow is more or less into the wind, release the mainsheet and hoist away, removing and stowing the boom crotch. The foot of the main should look like the illustration (175). If the main sets evenly, then hoist the jib and carry on (176).

Some skippers who want the option of point reefing feel that the points themselves offer too much wind resistance. So they reef by lacing a single, long line under the furled portion of the sail, up through a reefing eyelet, down under the sail, and so on. The only other lines used are the ones already mentioned for the tack and leech reef cringles.

172

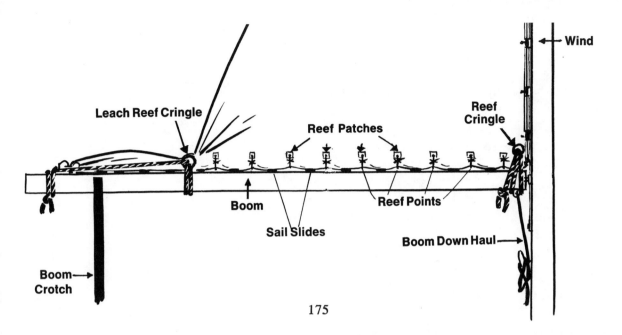

Leach Reef Cringle

Reef Cringle

Reef Patches

Wind

Boom

Reef Points

Sail Slides

Boom Down Haul

Boom
Crotch

175

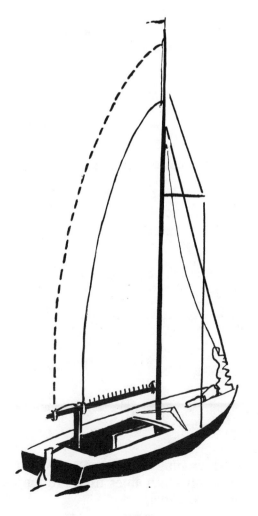

176

To shake out a tied-in reef, you work in exactly the reverse sequence of tying it in: lower the sail and secure the boom. Untie all the points (double check to make sure *all* of them are untied). Then release the clew and tack seizings (in that order), and hoist the sail to full height.

A recent development in reefing technique is *slab* or *jiffy* reefing. This system, which derives from point reefing, has speed as its main achievement; one loses the infinite adjustability of roller reefing.

A boat equipped for slab reefing usually has a fixed gooseneck and a set (or sometimes two) of reefing grommets. There may be no reef points, and in some cases only the tack and clew grommets are set in the sail.

By means of a tackle, a line led up from the boom, through the tack grommet, and back down is used to pull the mainsail tack down.

Someone will have to slack off the main halyard. The boom is then pulled up to the clew cringle by another line, which runs from a point on the boom aft of the reef cringle, through the cringle, back down to a cheek block on the boom and thence forward. The resulting large flake of sail may be left to flap or may be lashed up with reef points or lace line for neatness.

In recent years, a type of reefing that originated with large, cruising boats has spread to many (if not most) small craft. Called *roller reefing*, it's quicker and simpler than the point method; the gear involved is also more expensive and complex, and may fail in a pinch.

All the varieties of roller reefing work on the same basic principle: to reduce the area of the mainsail, it is simply rolled around its own revolving boom. Since the normal raised track and slides on a boom would chafe a rolled sail, roller booms have either a recessed track or groove-and-bolt-rope for the mainsail foot. For a well-setting roller reefed sail, the forward third of the boom should be tapered to about 60% of its maximum diameter.

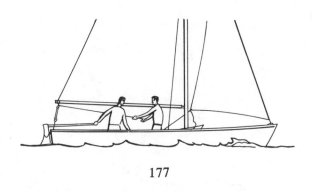

177

Reefing the main with the most common type of roller gear is very simple: while one man sails the boat under jib alone, the other slacks off the mainsheet just enough to maintain a reduced tension on the sail (177). With the main still pulling slightly, the crewman goes forward and slacks off the main halyard with one hand, while working the roller reefing crank with the other (178).

The tack of a roller reefing main is somewhat cut away, with its slides on an adjustable line; in this way the rolling sail stays clear of the gooseneck. The only critical part of the crewman's work is making sure that there's enough tension on the halyard so the sail rolls onto the boom tightly and evenly. Slides must be slipped off the track as they approach the boom.

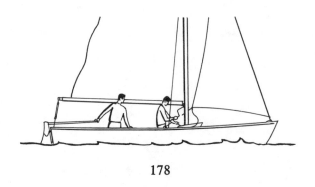

178

When the sail's area has been reduced enough, cleat the halyard, take in the mainsheet, and continue sailing (179). It may or may not be necessary to remove the lowest batten, depending on how deep the reef is, and whether or not there is an offset batten pocket.

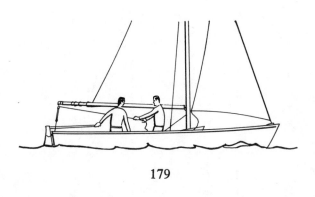

179

22: Emergency Handling in Squalls

Many small inshore sailboats aren't equipped for any sort of reefing. And whether a boat has reefing gear or not, her skipper should know how to handle her in heavy winds and seas, because these conditions can arise on any body of water with surprising swiftness.

If a squall or storm looms, keep an eye on

the boats to windward of you, since they'll receive the gusts first. Remember that squalls travel very fast, and can catch the unwary in seconds.

If wind puffs seem serious, luff up immediately and let the sheets run. Lower the board, if it isn't down already. If the squall seems likely to last more than a few minutes, put on life vests or preservers, drop the sails, main first, and get them off the deck, or at least tightly furled and stopped (180).

When in doubt, always drop the sails—it's a simple matter to raise them again. But if they're blown out, or the boat's capsized, you and your crew are in real trouble.

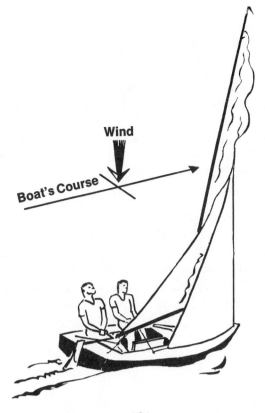

181

that could damage sails or battens. The skipper should be ready to let both sails run in a severe gust: don't, that is, cleat

180

In case of a real black squall, the boat will probably do best running before the wind under bare poles, if there is sea room enough to leeward. If the boat's going too fast, you can reduce her speed by trailing the anchor rode over the stern in a bight,* with one end made fast to each quarter.†

As the wind eases enough to permit setting some sail, even a boat without reefing gear has several choices:

1. Reach (usually the safest point of sailing) under taut jib and luffing main (181). The trick is to haul the jib in tight enough to backwind the main: in this way, the after portion of the main will hold enough wind to prevent the kind of savage flapping

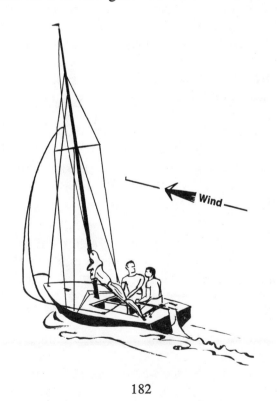

182

(*bight) *The part of a rope between the two ends, especially when it forms a curve or loop.*
†(quarter) *The upper parts of a boat's sides near the stern.*

the sheets down. This tactic works well in a puffy squall, where you can make good progress between the blasts.

2. If your boat can broad reach well under jib alone, try that (182). Some well-designed modern boats point quite high without a mainsail. Furl the main on its boom, which should be lashed in its crotch or to a deck fitting. Don't cleat the jib sheet, but hold it ready to let run.

3. Most sloops handle better under main alone, than with just the jib: of course, more sail is exposed (183). The boat will have considerable weather helm which is an added safety factor (though tiring to the helmsman). The crew should hike out during puffs, and luff the main if required.

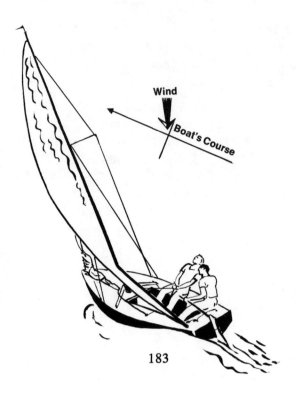

183

23: Knockdown and Capsize

Even the best-handled small sailboats can capsize, and sailing boards do it all the time. Most modern daysailers carry enough built-in flotation to keep the boat on the surface even when she's filled with water. And in any kind of serious weather, *skipper and crew should put on and fasten their life jackets before* the danger of knockdown or capsize becomes acute. It's very hard to don a life preserver properly while treading water, assuming the jacket doesn't drift off by itself.

In a *knockdown,* a sudden squall or wind shift heels the boat so much that the sails may be immersed and water pours into the cockpit (184). Swift action on the part of skipper and crew may avert any further mishap.

As soon as the boat heels to a dangerous degree, put the helm down (to leeward), luff up, and let the sheets run. If the rudder still has enough bite on the water, the boat may round up, and a keel boat will usually pull herself up—thanks to the righting moment* of her ballast—once the pressure is off the sails.

But a boat that's over on her side with no righting moment—a centerboard boat, for instance—is said to be *capsized*: left to herself, she will simply remain in that position.

When a boat capsizes, there are several important steps to take:

1. Count heads: make sure all hands are present; if someone has been hit on the head or is trapped under the boat, you must know it right away.

2. Stay with the boat: if life jackets haven't been donned, even good swimmers must put them on now.

3. Capture loose gear: floorboards, fenders, and the like can float away quickly if not secured. Stuff equipment in a sailbag tied to the boat, if you can.

*(righting moment) *Leverage exerted by the ballast and hull form: once extraordinary pressures—such as the sail's being immersed—are removed from the rigging, a properly designed keel boat will resume an upright position. Most keel boats are not fitted with flotation, and would sink if the hull were filled.*

4. Get the sails down: release the main and jib halyards (making sure the bitter ends are secured), and pull the sails down the mast and forestay.* Furl them loosely—this

is one time neatness doesn't count—and secure all other loose lines.

5. Lower the centerboard: if it's not already down. One or two crew members can stand on the board and grab the gunwale, leaning backward to exert a righting force on the boat. If the board has been sharpened, no one should stand on it barefoot. A crew member with a life jacket can swim around

* *Under some conditions, such as in a race with a trained crew with a small boat and lightweight rig, the boat can be righted with the sails up, as shown above. Generally it is necessary to lower the sails.*

to the mast and push up on it—every little bit helps (185).

The boat should begin to raise by herself. When she gets upright, she will be unwieldy and very unstable, and should be boarded over the transom. Get the salvaged gear aboard. If the centerboard trunk is capped, you can begin to bail; if the trunk's open at the top, you'll have to plug it—clothing

185

will do well enough, but a regular trunk cap isn't a bad thing to have for such emergencies.

In severely choppy water, bailing a swamped boat by hand is often impossible. The crew must simply conserve their energy and wait for help. Get in the boat and begin to signal in one of the accepted ways listed below:

1. Hand-held flare or orange smoke signal.

2. Distress flag.

3. Horn, whistle, or other sound-producing device: give five or more short, distinct blasts in series.

4. Manual signal—if the boat is stable enough, stand facing the potential rescuers, with your arms fully extended at shoulder height. Raise and lower arms repeatedly. Whenever you have to make a signal of distress, do it wholeheartedly: even a swamped sailboat may not appear to be in trouble unless a passing skipper's attention is fully attracted (186).

As a rescuer comes alongside, don't let him get too close until you're sure there are no loose lines that can foul his propeller. He should come up to leeward of you, and assist the wet and tired crew aboard. Be sure engines are stopped, not just in neutral, when taking persons from the water.

If you're to be towed, take a line from the

186

towboat, lead it through the bow chocks, and make it fast to the most secure fitting. If your mooring cleat isn't sufficiently heavy (or properly through-bolted*), the towline can be made fast around the base of the mast, being careful to avoid projecting fittings that might chafe the line.

One of the crew should remain aboard the swamped but righted boat, to keep weight aft and to steer. A swamped boat should be towed very, very slowly—water weighs 64 lbs. per cubic foot, and its surge can tear a boat apart.

If a boat must be towed on its side—a last resort—speed should be dead slow. Before trying to tow a capsized boat, see if you can't remove the mast, boom, and stays: it's not easy to do in the water, but with the top hamper off, any boat should be rightable.

*(through-bolted) *Where possible, all a boat's fittings should be bolted through the planking, with the bolts running through an additional backing block to spread the load, and secured with large-diameter washers and nuts.*

24: Man Overboard

There's seldom any excuse for a man's falling off a small boat. But it does happen, it's no joke, and the skipper should know instantly what to do.

1. Keep sight of the man in the water: a human head is small and hard to see, especially when the surface is a mass of whitecaps. If possible, assign one crew member to watch the man overboard while you maneuver to pick him up (187).

2. Heave a life preserver—a soft one— near the man's head, but not at it, and slightly to windward.

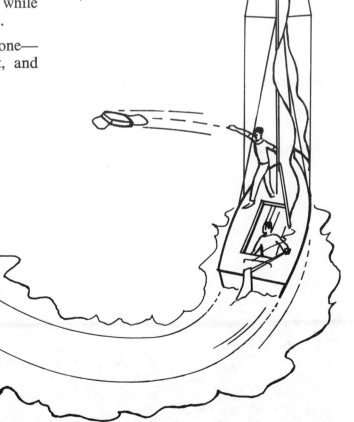

187

3. Before trying to pick the man up, be sure that the boat is fully under control. Often a man goes overboard in the course of a crisis. Resolve the crisis aboard first, or you're likely to have more than one person in trouble.

4. Approach the man in the water as if he were a mooring buoy, but with the aim of laying the boat dead in the water alongside him, and slightly to windward.

5. If the man cannot climb aboard by himself, get a line secured around his chest, under the arms, so he cannot slip away. Then ease him in over the gunwale (188).

188

25: Dismasting

Earlier, accidental jibing was mentioned as a common cause of dismasting, but there are others: a chafed stay, rot in the spar, or simply an extra-powerful gust of wind —all *can* snap the mast. Fortunately for today's sailors, modern materials have made mast and rigging failures less frequent than they once were.

Masts do break, and the accident is both nerve-wracking and dangerous, if not quite as disastrous as it may seem at the time. As in most nautical crises, the man who keeps his head is likely to escape with the least damage to boat and rigging.

Masts are most likely to fail where there's great stress, inherent weakness, or both. That's why so many broken masts have snapped at or just below the spreaders (189), where the force of the shrouds is concentrated, or at the level of the boom. In both these places, stress is combined with a number of fittings attached to—often weakening—the spar.

If your mast fails, the first thing to do is prevent further damage: the spar itself is probably wrecked for good, but the sails, rigging, and fittings may all be reclaimed. In addition, a toppled mast attached to the boat by stays can easily damage the hull or even sink you.

1. Try to get the mast, sails, and boom aboard where you can work on them. It may be necessary to cast loose the standing rigging to do this: removing the cotter pins or rings from the turnbuckle toggles is the best and least destructive way of freeing the rigging.

2. Few if any daysailers carry wire cutters aboard. Except as a last resort, don't let any "helper" snip your standing rigging: it will be useless afterwards.

3. Get the sails off and stowed, to prevent them from being snagged and ripped (190).

4. If the mast has snapped at the spreaders, it may be possible to use the base of it as a *jury rig,** assuming that you haven't an auxiliary engine, and there's no help in the offing. On a shortened mast, the foot of the sail may be abbreviated enough to go up the track (191). You should be able

191

to sail an easy reach, the boat will be steadier with some sail up, and its appearance should certainly attract help.

5. Lash down all unused spars, broken or intact, so the fittings can be salvaged later.

190

*(jury rig) *Any makeshift or emergency rig contrived by the crew to replace something that has carried away.*

Part VI: Sailor's Seamanship

An introductory book like this cannot teach all the complex elements of seamanship, but this section will discuss some things every boatman should know before he ventures away from the mooring.

26: Line and Knots

Far more than the powerboat skipper, the sailor depends on line of various types. The most common varieties encountered by the small boat sailor are:

1. Nylon: made of synthetic fiber and used for anchor, mooring and dock lines. It's characterized by great strength, resistance to rot, and considerable stretch under load. Because of this last characteristic, nylon is not suitable for halyards or sheets.

2. Dacron: another line made from artificial fibers. Not quite as strong as nylon, Dacron is equally resistant to rot. It has relatively little stretch, and so is used for sheets and for those halyards where a small degree of stretch is allowable.

3. Manila: best all-around line made from natural fibers, and it comes in several qualities. It will rot if stowed wet, or in a wet place, and it's not nearly as strong as nylon or Dacron.

4. Polypropylene: another synthetic, identifiable by its slippery texture. It floats, and is thus very useful for dinghy towlines and mooring pickup lines.

Sailors' line comes in two basic styles—*laid* and *braided*. Laid line is made by twisting fibers into yarns, several of which go to make up a strand; most rope is three-strand, and because of the direction in which it spirals, is called right-hand lay (192).

Laid is generally less costly than braided line (193), which is made up of an inner and outer part. Braid is more difficult to splice, but is easier to run through sheaves (and human hands), and is thus especially favored for sheets and halyards. A new development in braid, of interest to sailors, is braided sheet and halyard line dyed in any one of a variety of colors, to enable a sailor to tell, say, a coiled halyard from a coiled sheet.

193

192

In the great days of sail, a good seaman had literally hundreds of knots, bends, hitches and splices to call upon. While the modern sailor may well find pleasure in mastering as many knots as possible, there are really only a few that he *must* know. A sailor should literally be able to tie these with his eyes closed.

1. Figure Eight: this is called a *stopper*, since it is used at the bitter end of a line, to keep it from running out through a block or fairlead. Most commonly used at the ends of sheets (194).

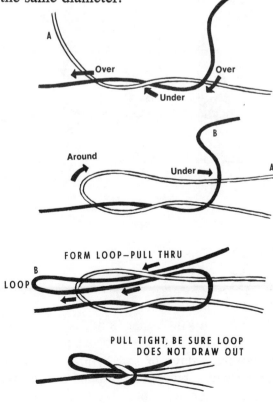

194

2. The Slippery Reef: in old times, the reef knot was used in reefing—hence the name—but a variant, the *Slippery Reef* knot, (195) is better for brief use: it may be too slippery! A square knot (197a) should only be used when both pieces of line are the same diameter.

Over Over
Under

Around
Under A

FORM LOOP—PULL THRU
LOOP B

PULL TIGHT, BE SURE LOOP
DOES NOT DRAW OUT

195

3. The Sheet Bend: a far better way to join lines, as it won't jam, is easy to tie, and works equally well no matter what the respective sizes of the two lines (196). The *Double Sheet Bend* is even more secure (197). Remember, the larger of two odd-sized lines should form the loop, as shown in (197), for either single or double sheet bend.

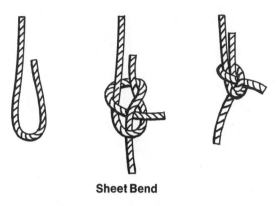

Sheet Bend

196

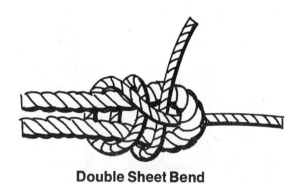

Double Sheet Bend

197

4. The Reverse Surgeon's Knot (198) is the most secure way of creating a knot that resists shaking loose, but that can be untied later. It consists simply of a square knot with an extra turn in the upper half-knot. The regular surgeon's knot was invented to make secure ties in surgical suture material, and is often used in knotting plastic leader material.

5. The Bowline (199): if a landsman were asked to name one sailor's knot, chances are he'd come up with the bowline nine times out of ten. It is an excellent knot because it stays tied, won't jam, and is easy to untie. Any time a temporary loop at the end of a line is called for, the bowline is a suitable response.

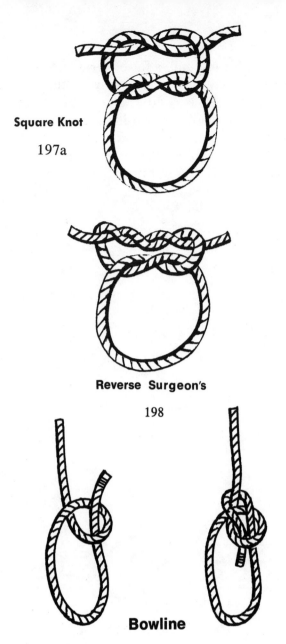

Square Knot

197a

Reverse Surgeon's

198

Bowline

199

6. Clove Hitch: though not a secure attachment—it can be worked loose by repeatedly varying the angle of pull—the clove hitch is a very convenient way of making a line fast temporarily to a piling (200). If left alone, it should be secured by adding one or two half hitches around the standing part.

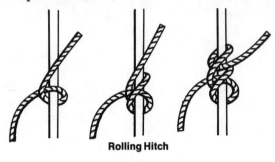

Clove Hitch

200

7. Rolling Hitch: for length-wise pull along a spar, the specialized rolling hitch has no competitors (201).

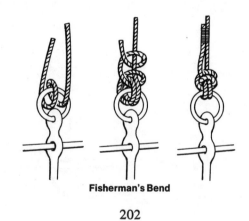

Rolling Hitch

201

8. Fisherman's Bend: also called an *Anchor Bend*, it's usually used to make the anchor rode fast to the ring or shackle of an anchor (202). The bitter end should be led back and *seized* (as illustrated) to the standing part if the anchor is to be left for more than an hour or two.

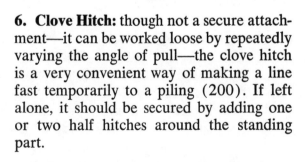

Fisherman's Bend

202

27: Seizing, Whipping and Splicing

A *seizing* is merely a binding of light line around two segments of heavier line. It keeps a knot or bend—especially in new, inflexible line—from working itself free. Waterproof tape is also suitable.

Whipping, on the other hand, is a method of treating the bitter end of a line to keep it from unraveling (203). Synthetic lines of small diameter can be whipped simply by burning the ends with a match: the nylon

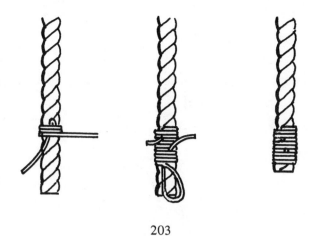

203

or Dacron will melt and then solidify into a hard knob. Waterproof tape will make a serviceable, if un-nautical, temporary whipping. A liquid whipping of plastic is also available: the end of the line is simply dipped into the material, which hardens and forms a permanent coating. And a thermally-activated plastic collar can be slipped over the end of the line and heated until it shrinks to a tight fit.

But the old-fashioned whipping is far more decorative when properly done, and it's not difficult.

1. Lay a bight of waxed sail twine (or whipping thread) along the rope to be whipped, with the closed end of the loop toward the end of the line, and about an inch from it (204).

2. With the standing part of the twine, lay a series of tight, even turns around the rope

and the twine loop. Leave enough of the twine's bitter end protruding so that it can be grabbed with the fingers.

3. The whipping should be at least as long as the diameter of the rope being whipped. Cut the standing part of the twine and feed the end through the loop remaining.

4. While holding the twine-and-loop in place with a fingertip, pull the bitter end that was left protruding in step two. It will draw the loop and the end under the whipping.

5. When the loop and extra end have fully disappeared, cut the pulling end of the twine as close to the whipping as possible. Pass a match flame over the whipping just close enough to melt the wax on the twine and make it run together.

Splicing

There are two splices of importance to the small boat sailor, the *eye* splice and *short* splice.

Eye Splice: this makes a permanent loop in the end of a line, with a minimum loss of strength in the rope itself. Practice splicing with a length of manila ⅜ or ½ inch in diameter—synthetic fiber lines tend to unlay themselves very quickly, unless manipulated with some skill.

1. Unlay the line for about 8 inches. Tape

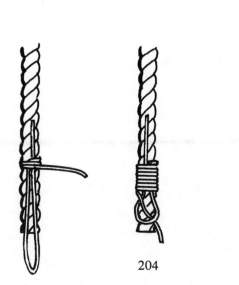

204

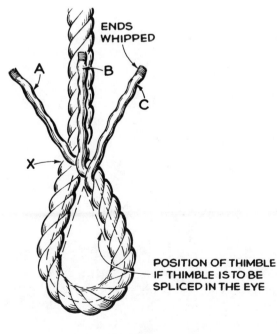

ENDS WHIPPED

A   B

C

X

POSITION OF THIMBLE
IF THIMBLE IS TO BE
SPLICED IN THE EYE

205

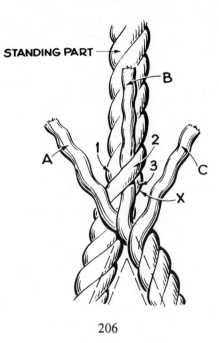

STANDING PART

206

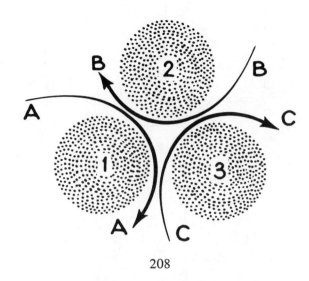

208

the ends of the three strands to keep them from losing shape. Also tape the main body of the line to keep it from unlaying further.

2. Bring the unlaid working end up to the right of the standing part to form a loop of the size you want. Open the rope with a *fid* or *marlinspike* to form the apertures for the tucks, all of which are made *against* the lay (from right to left), across the twist of the rope (205).

3. Hold the working part so the three unlaid strands are side by side; now tuck the center strand under a strand of the standing part (206).

4. Now tuck the strand to the left of the center strand *over* the strand holding the first tuck in place, and *under* the next strand beyond (207).

5. Turn the loop with its two tucks over. The final tuck will have only one place to go, but make sure that this tuck goes from right to left: this is where most splices go wrong (208).

6. The first series of tucks is complete; draw each one tight, strand by strand. Now take any one of the three strands and begin the second series of tucks: the rule to remember is *over* one strand and *under* the next. After each series of three tucks, draw

207

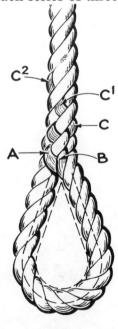

209

the strands tight so the strain remains even. With manila line, three tucks of each strand —three full series of tucks—is sufficient. The more slippery synthetics will require five series of tucks.

The finished splice can be rolled under foot or between the palms for a smooth appearance. Cut off the protruding ends about half an inch from the splice and singe them (if the line is synthetic). Remove the tape around the neck of the splice, which should now look like this (209).

Short Splice: for permanently joining two lines of equal diameter and the same material, a short splice leaves the lines as

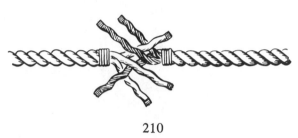

210

strong as possible. Since it increases the diameter of the finished line, a short splice can't be used where a line must run through a block. There is a splice for this application, the so-called *long splice,* but it weakens the line so much that one is usually better off getting a new length of rope.

1. Begin as with the eye splice, by unlaying each of the lines for about eight inches and taping the ends. Marry the two lines, by placing them together, unlaid end to unlaid end, in such a way that the strands of one line alternate with those of the other (210).

2. Seize the married lines in place with a piece of twine, using three or four turns (211).

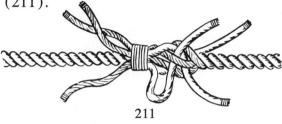

211

3. Begin the tucks, as with the eye splice, making all three tucks of a series in one piece of line, then turning the splice end for end and making the three-tuck series in the other line.

4. When a sufficient number of tucks is made for the type of line, finish the loose strands as with the eye splice, and remove the whipping (212).

212

The Ditty Bag

To deal with splicing, whipping, minor sail repair, and the like, a skipper should have a *ditty bag* with a few basic tools and spares. The illustration (213) shows one such bag, with its contents spread out for display: marlinspike fid, sailmaker's palm, beeswax, sail needles, waxed whipping twine, Dacron sail thread, pocket knife, waterproof tape (narrow for whipping, wide for sail repair). (Photo courtesy of West Products, Inc.)

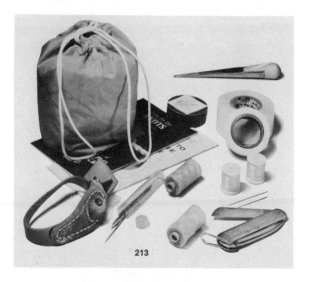

213

28: Coiling and Heaving Line

Coiling loose line for stowage is somewhat different from the coil of a halyard shown earlier (see p. 38). The illustrations show three different methods of coiling lines. The first method is the most common, and this coil will stay orderly in a locker even when mixed in with other gear (214). The sec-

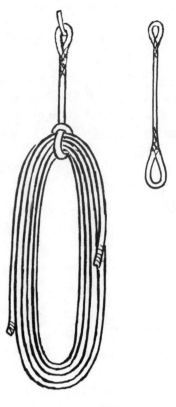

216

ond method (215), which takes a little longer to make and unmake, is for line that must be tossed and handled while coiled: it will survive a good deal of stirring about. The final method (216) shows how a coiled sheet (for instance) can be hung in place secured by a loop—shock cord is best.

Heaving a line is definitely a good sailor's accomplishment. It is not as easy as it looks, and there are a few methods for making it successful.

1. Always use a line considerably longer than the distance it must be thrown—half again as long is about the minimum.

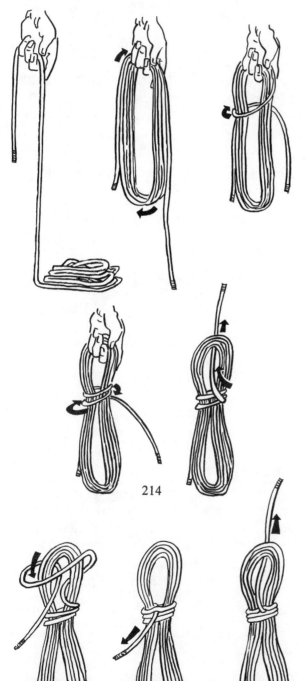

214

Coiling

215

217

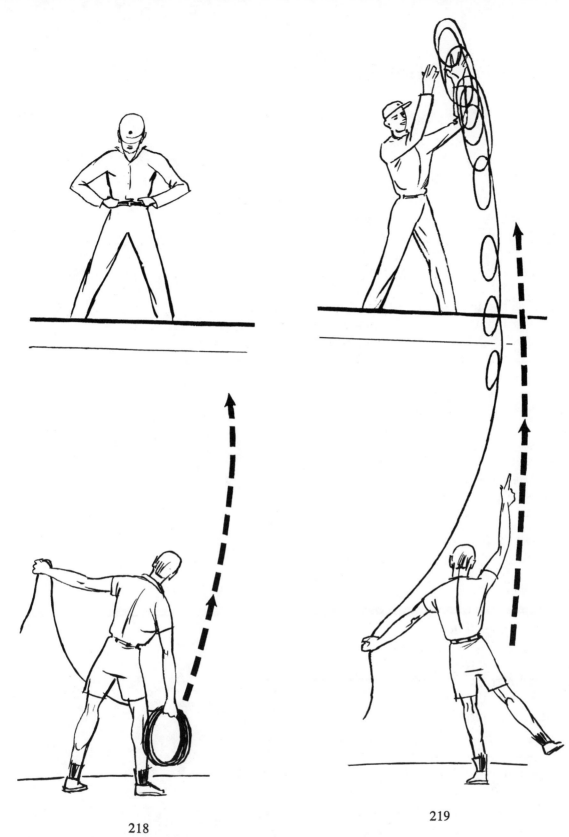

218

219

2. Coil the line carefully and evenly in small loops that will feed out easily (217).

3. Hold the coil in the throwing hand at arm's length, with the free end in the other hand. Throw the coil with an underhand swing (218). The coil should be released so that its trajectory will take it to the receiver's head. If necessary, first throw a light "messenger" line with a weighted monkey's fist at its end. If the size and length of line becomes too much to swing in one hand, carry about half the coil loosely on the palm of the non-throwing hand so the line will run out easily after the half which is thrown has reached its full extension.

29: Maintenance

The maintenance of boats is a book-length subject in itself. Information given here is intended for only the beginner's guidance, and as a bare minimum to keep a boat clean and healthy.

1. Hull: the hull of a modern fiberglass sailboat needs very little attention, compared to that of a wood boat of the same size. It does, however, require some care. The exterior should be waxed at least once a month, using any of the preparations developed for marine use. Varnished wood brightwork should be washed with clean, fresh water at the end of every sail, and dried with a chamois.

The underbody should be painted with a good grade of anti-fouling paint if the boat will remain at moorings or at a pier. In warm water areas, the skipper should scrub down the hull below the waterline at least twice a season anyway, to remove the scum and growths the anti-fouling paint hasn't repelled.

2. Metal fittings: the metal parts of the boat—cleats, blocks, mast and boom—should be preserved from rust and corrosion. Even the most resistant metal will suffer somewhat in salt water, so the metalwork should be sluiced off with fresh water at the end of every sail. The best metals for marine use are titanium, bronze, stainless steel, and marine alloys of aluminum. Keep moving parts lightly oiled or greased, according to manufacturer recommendations.

3. Sails and lines: remember that all artificial fibers break down under strong, prolonged sunlight, so stow lines and sails in a shady, well-ventilated, dry place. Make sure that sails and lines rub no more than necessary against fittings and rigging, and try to arrange some form of chafe gear wherever rubbing is unavoidable. Genoas and jib sheets usually chafe on the shrouds: rollers (220) can be rigged at small cost to minimize this chafe. The outer ends of spreaders all attack overlapping headsails, and these small spars should be fitted with chafing gear to protect the sails (221).

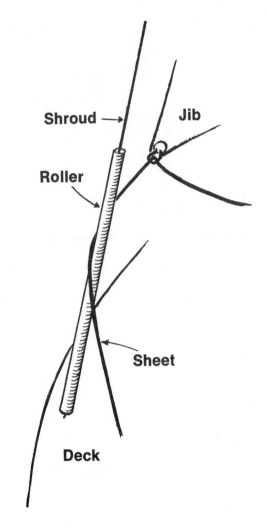

220

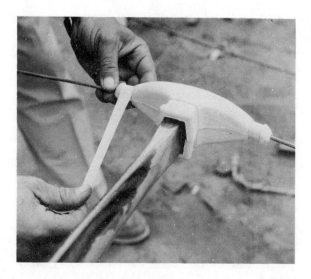

221

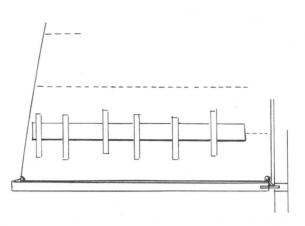

223

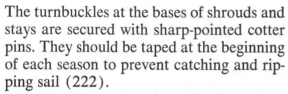

222

If a sail does rip, it should be repaired by a sailmaker. In an emergency, special waterproof sail tape can be used to make a temporary repair. Apply it as in the diagram (223), and don't subject the sail to any more strain than absolutely necessary.

The turnbuckles at the bases of shrouds and stays are secured with sharp-pointed cotter pins. They should be taped at the beginning of each season to prevent catching and ripping sail (222).

Part VII—30: Guide to Buying Sails

Buying a sail has all the elements of buying an engine or buying a new suit of clothes. A sail must, after all, fit the boat and supply the necessary drive, but a sail is not a piece of hardware. Making sails is still partially art, an art liberally laced with style and fashion.

The analogy goes further. Clothes are either ready-made or custom tailored. So are sails. A few years ago, all sails were made singly in individual lofts all over the country. Today, however, a number of production sailmakers produce quantities of identical sails for many popular models and classes of boats.

If you have one of these standard boats—or are thinking of buying one—you then have a choice: ordering sails custom designed from the fabric up by a sailmaker, or buying a set of production sails from the boat's builder or from his dealer. As with custom clothes versus ready-made, the choice depends on relative cost, relative quality, and the availability of after-sale service.

Production sails offer the advantage of cheapness, but (particularly in the case of foreign sails) the sails may be of less than first quality. And, if there is something wrong with the sail, getting it adjusted is difficult since the buyer must return it to a dealer who sends it either to the boat builder (who sends it on to the sailmaker) or directly to the sailmaker. In each case, there is no direct contact between the buyer and the sailmaker.

With custom sails there is plenty of personal contact between one and the other, and quick and satisfactory adjustments of poorly fitting sails are easy to accomplish —provided the sailmaker is a person of integrity and has the desire to please.

However, custom sails *do* cost more. In most cases, though, they do not cost that much more than ready-made sails. Production sails are usually marketed through builders and their dealers. Each one adds on a profit. The result is that the ready-made price is close to or even equal to the custom price.

For the truth of the matter is that a sail made of American Dacron will not wear out. More correctly, the Dacron itself will not wear out. Stitching will chafe and give way, but the fabric itself seems to go on forever. Therefore, it makes sense to pay a little more at the beginning and have something that will last as long as you're willing to take care of it.

Sails for Small Boats

There is actually, in the smaller sizes, little difference, if any, in fabric or manufacturing techniques between sails made for racing or just for sailing, nor should you seriously consider buying anything but a first-class sail capable of racing. Not only will the boat perform better if you do in fact only sail her, but you can move into racing later without buying new sails—and reselling the boat will be easier.

In smaller boats deciding what sails to buy is usually very simple. If the boat in question has a class organization, that organization has already probably decided for you what sails are allowable. In this latter case, you have no decision at all to make: you merely order what the class allows, usually a main, a working jib and a spinnaker. In some few classes, a genoa is also permitted.

The minimum weight of fabric is usually specified, too, and it is normally wise to stay with the minimum weight—even for day sailing. There is strength to spare in even the lightest Dacron, and a light sail will be easier to handle. Some Dacron fabrics are "softer" than others, meaning that they have not been so rigorously heat-set. A "hard" Dacron is a stiff piece of goods, and some will advise people against it—except for maximum performance. It is my feeling, however, that—at least in the lighter weights—the hardest Dacron will not be too awkward to handle, and a sail made of it will keep its shape far longer.

If your boat, or the boat you are considering, doesn't belong to a class, you will have some latitude. The accompanying chart will indicate the general range of weights and, again, it is my own feeling that it is better to stay on the light side. Consult your sailmaker.

A main, of course, will be essential and I feel that it should be cut to the maximum possible size.

One jib of moderate area—somewhere between the biggest possible and an underfed working jib—will probably suffice, especially if the main can be reduced in area quickly. Two jibs would be better, with one larger—maximum or nearly so, and one a working jib—or smaller. The second jib may spend ninety percent of its life in the sail bag, but the few times it's needed make it worth ten times its original cost. Certainly, if money is available for a third sail, and the debate is between a spinnaker and a small jib—and even a storm trysail— I'd opt for the heavy weather sails. The purchase of a spinnaker for a day-sailing or cruising boat is a luxury that can be indefinitely postponed.

Sails for Larger Boats

As the boat size increases, the question of what sails to purchase and what they should be made of becomes increasingly complicated. Some of the factors to consider are: Where will boat be used? For what primary purpose? If she is to be raced, under what measurement rule? What will constitute the normal cruising crew? How much money is available?

For simplicity's sake, let's take one 30-odd-foot auxiliary and look at how her inventory grew. When she was first purchased, the owner was new to sailing, had a youngster for help, and had a fairly limited budget. Minimum inventory was indicated, composed of a main and what is variously called a lapper, mule or #3 genoa. By whatever name, this is a jib that is larger than a working jib, overlaps the mast a bit and provides better performance while still being easy to handle. A reasonable alternative would have been a larger roller furling jib, a subject we will discuss later.

The crew of this boat grew a bit, money became more available and the owner became more confident. The first addition was the workhorse of the modern auxiliary: the #1 genoa. #1 genoas today are designated by the percentage figures 150%, 170%, or 180%. These numbers refer to the ratio between the length of a line drawn perpendicular to the luff of the jib, between the luff and the clew, and the length of the foredeck. Thus a 150% genoa has an LP (luff perpendicular) that is 150% of the foredeck length.

Which size #1 genoa you buy will depend on where the boat will be used and what rule the boat races under. The matter is subject to an endless debate that is well beyond the scope of this chapter.

Serious entry into racing requires a spinnaker—one spinnaker at least. Nylon is universally used for spinnakers, but they can be cut a number of different ways depending on whether they will be used for running or reaching, for heavy air or light wind. The first spinnaker should probably be deep rather than broad. This will limit its reaching usefulness, but it will be easier to set and keep full in light air—and will be more stable when it blows. The reaching chute can come later.

Along with the spinnaker—or soon after—comes the cheater or, more properly, the spinnaker staysail, a small nylon sail set under the chute to fill up the hole always left when the spinnaker lifts. Today, these have become sophisticated sails, too, and once again a full examination of the relative merits of the various types, the tall-boys and the regular-cut ones, is out of order here.

An extended discussion of how extensive a racing auxiliary's inventory can become also is out of order, but it could conceivably, in addition to everything already mentioned, have light and heavy #1 genoas; #2, #3 and 4 genoas, a working jib, storm trysail and storm jib, and a reacher and/or a drifter. All this in addition to a mainsail which can become, with the most intense racers, a study in itself.

Cruising Sails

Sails on cruising boats are simple in comparison and they *are* different on larger boats. While a large racing boat has a crew that can handle "hard" Dacron sails, the limited crew on a cruising boat will be far happier with soft Dacron. This is still not very soft, but it does handle more easily and it will keep its stitching intact far longer. Not to mention ladies' fingernails.

The true blue-water cruising boat will have working sails cut vertically, with no battens, and no roach, but the sails will be roped on luff and foot and taped on the leech, and be well-fitted with chafing patches. Inshore, weekend cruising boats do not need to go to these extremes. Regular working sails of soft Dacron will perform better and last well.

A cruising boat's inventory will be much

smaller than her racing sister's. It will be composed of working sails, plus perhaps a large genoa for light airs. It will definitely include storm canvas.

Reefing

Easy reefing—and easy sail handling in general—is even more essential with short-handed cruising boats than with racing boats. Mainsail roller reefing is a must, and roller furling (and reefing?) of headsails is gaining popularity, although it has its controversies.

These are basically two in number. The first deals with the jib when partially furled, or reefed; in my opinion, it is a terrible setting sail. Some people don't seem to mind, but there is no question in my mind that a big jib, cut for moderate airs, is far too baggy for heavy wind when partially furled.

The second difficulty is avoidable and concerns the use of the jib's luff wire as a headstay, a practice some recommend. I flatly disagree: eliminating the separate headstay puts the entire load of the rig, and the safety of the boat, on the luff of the jib—dangerous to begin with. But the worst thing about this system is the difficulty in making repairs to the jib—a piece of fabric that will, after all, part a seam sooner or later. To stitch a sail that is firmly attached to the *only* thing holding the mast up is a major yard job involving a full gang of riggers. If the jib is on a separate wire, it can simply be lowered like a regular jib and trundled off to the sail loft.

The last paragraph implied that you can expect sails to fall apart, which isn't quite accurate. To be truthful, sail stitching is still a problem for *all* sailmakers. Even soft Dacron is hard; the stitching lies on the surface instead of burying itself as it used to in cotton sails. This makes it vulnerable to chafe.

Since Dacron fabric itself is nearly indestructable, the wise sailor will therefore buy sails from the fellow who a) does his best to find and use the most chafe resistant thread, b) builds the sail carefully for maximum durability, c) will be happy to give your sails a seasonal examination for incipient problems, and d) does his best to get you sailing again if you do run into trouble.

Fortunately, the sailmaker who does one of these things does them all.

[*Note:* Herbert Hild, the author of this chapter, is a well-known East Coast sailmaker.]

Simple Sail Plan: the literature accompanying a stock boat nearly always contains a sail plan, like this one for a small cruising auxiliary. Usual practice is to show centers of effort of the individual sails and of the sail plan itself, areas of the mainsail and the foretriangle (*not necessarily* the area of any individual jib), and several measurements of primary interest to handicap racers. In this drawing, J stands for the horizontal distance from the tack to the forward side of the mast (or its downward extension, as marked here by the small + in the cabin window); B is the maximum foot of the mainsail from a black band on the outer end of the boom to the after side of the mast; P is the maximum mainsail luff, measured from the black band at the top of the mast to another slightly above the deck. P_2 the vertical measurement from deck level to the intersection of mast and highest jib stay *or* highest eye or strop for headsail or spinnaker halyard, whichever is greater. Dotted outlines indicate sizes of standard sails, in this case jib, genoa, and reacher. These are CCA rule designations; IOR rule differs.

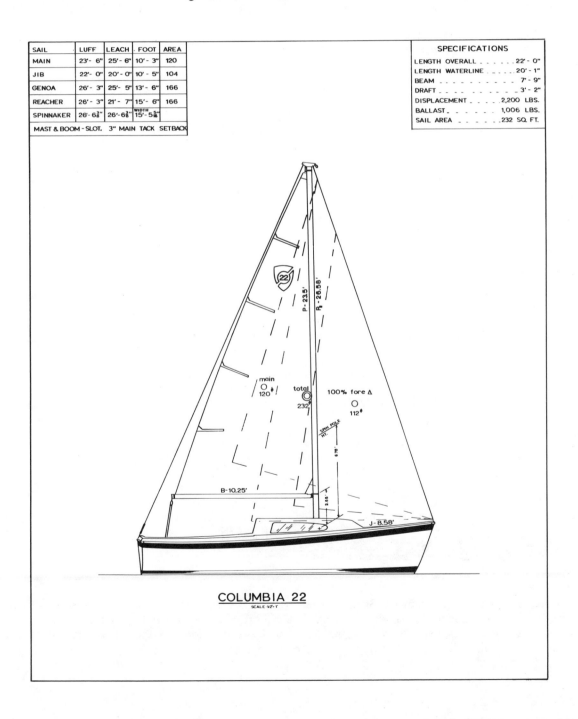

SAIL	LUFF	LEACH	FOOT	AREA
MAIN	23'- 6"	25'- 6"	10'- 3"	120
JIB	22'- 0"	20'- 0"	10'- 5"	104
GENOA	26'- 3"	25'- 5"	13'- 6"	166
REACHER	26'- 3"	21'- 7"	15'- 6"	166
SPINNAKER	26'-6⅜"	26'-6⅜"	WIDTH 15'- 5⅜"	

MAST & BOOM - SLOT. 3" MAIN TACK SETBACK

SPECIFICATIONS

LENGTH OVERALL	22'- 0"
LENGTH WATERLINE	20'- 1"
BEAM	7'- 9"
DRAFT	3'- 2"
DISPLACEMENT	2,200 LBS.
BALLAST	1,006 LBS.
SAIL AREA	232 SQ. FT.

COLUMBIA 22

SCALE ½"-1'

BOAT SIZE	TABLE OF SAIL CLOTH WEIGHTS							
	Main	Working Jib	#1 Genoa	#2 Genoa	#3 Genoa	Storm Sails	Spinnaker	Light reachers, etc.
Smallest, to 14'	3 oz.	3 oz.	—	—	—	—	¾ oz.	Either 1½ oz. Nylon or 2 oz. Dacron*
15-18	3-4	3-4	3	—	—	—	¾	
20-25	4½-5	4½-5	3½-4	5	6	6½	½-1.2	
30-35	6	6	4½	6	7¾	7	½-1.2	
40-45	7-7½	7-7½	5-6	6½-7	7¾	8	½-1.5	
50	8	8	6-7	7½	8		¾-1.5	

* Lightest Dacron commercially available.
Weights of U. S. sails are in ounces per yard of cloth 28½″ wide.

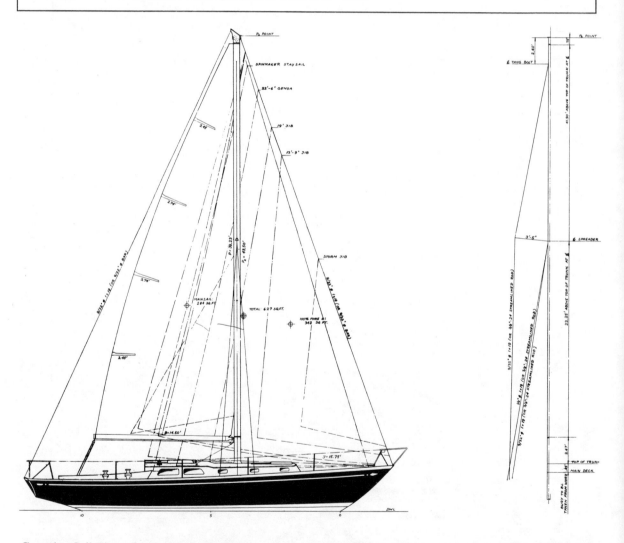

Complex Sail Plan: this Sparkman & Stephens ocean racer was designed for a complete and sophisticated suit of sails. In addition to the basic measurements, the draftsman has also indicated the lengths of the battens and the size and type of wire rigging. The line inside the forestay represents the luff of the spinnaker staysail, which is set flying, not snapped to a stay.

31: Daysailers and One-Designs

Though the racer-cruisers may be more glamorous, it's a safe bet that sailboats without cruising accommodations will continue to dominate American sailing—at least in numbers—for some years to come.

For one thing, there's the matter of cost—thanks to modern materials like Dacron, nylon, fiberglass and aluminum, the small sailboat today is about as inexpensive to maintain as a boat could be, and mass production has helped keep purchase prices down to a sane level.

While a racing sailor may well need a complex sail wardrobe, the man who simply wants to get out on the water in a sailboat will require only one or two sails to do it. And these sails, properly treated, will last far longer than cotton sails did.

It would seem that there'd be a basic difference between sailboats designed to race and those meant to potter around the harbor, but it doesn't work out that way. Since daysailers and one-designs race against each other, *any* daysailer can be a racer, which is not true of boats like distance racers, which are really running against a handicap system. Of course, many one-design aficionados want only the fastest and most sophisticated boat for themselves—as one of them said, "You don't race Edsels, you race Maseratis." Still, any sailboat can race, and most can potter, too.

The real difference is between *class* and *model:* a model is a manufacturer's proprietary design, built by him alone; a class, on the other hand, is a group of similar (often nearly identical) boats which may be built by several different builders. The class is organized to permit racing within the group on an even-up basis. Stars, Lightnings, Snipes—all of these are class boats, and to be more precise, they are *one-design* class boats. This term simply means that the organization has set down standard specifications to ensure that the boats called Lightnings (or Stars, or Snipes) are as close to identical as possible.

The other type of class, exemplified by Moths or 12-meter sloops, is the *development* group, in which boats also race without time allowance. Development boats differ within a class, but each boat has to fit within a measurement formula that takes into account such things as displacement, ballast, dimensions, and sail area, balancing one factor off against the others.

Some proprietary boats—the Sunfish is perhaps the best example—have developed extraordinarily large and successful class organizations, with national and even international scope.

If there is any difference between a boat that's primarily a racer and one that isn't, it's that the racing craft is likely to make concessions in comfort for the sake of performance. A smaller cockpit, for instance, or a mainsheet traveler located for sailing efficiency spang in the middle of things. Some few racing boats, like the Flying Dutchman, are so highly bred that they are not intended for hacking around at all.

But for your first sailboat, you're probably best advised to get a boat with racing potential, and more especially, with a local racing fleet. There are two good reasons: first, you yourself will almost certainly want to try racing at some point, and if you don't, your children will; second, a strong racing class in the area means that when you move on to another boat, your present one will be that much easier to sell.

One word of warning: if you buy a boat that's part of a racing class, don't make any irrevocable alterations that will make her ineligible to race with her sisters—unless you plan to take a loss when you come to sell. Your chances of improving on the work of a competent naval architect are not great, and if you have carefully calculated the numbers and talents of the potential crew, and the waters in which the boat will be used, you should have no difficulty finding a boat to suit your tastes and your purse. Finally, be sure to choose a boat with *positive flotation*—one that will float and support her crew even when filled with water.

Newport 16—Basically a daysailer with overnight accommodations for two. LOA 15′7″ / LWL 13′8″ / Beam 6′3″ / Draft 2′-3′9″ / Sail Area 137 sq. ft. / Displacement 650 lbs.

O'Day Widgeon—A popular family trainer in fiberglass. LOA 12′4″ / LWL 11′6″ / Beam 5′8″ / Draft 5″-3′6″ / Sail Area 90 sq. ft. / Weight 250 lbs.

Atlantic—A traditional one-design with a new lease on life thanks to fiberglass construction. LOA 30′7″ / LWL 21′6″ / Beam 6′6″ / Draft 4′9″ / Sail Area 367 sq. ft. / Displacement 4,559 lbs.

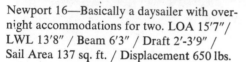

Hobie Cat 14—A relatively new multihull racing class. LOA 14′ / Beam 7′8″ / Draft 8″ / Sail Area 110 sq. ft. / Weight 215 lbs.

32: Small Racer-Cruisers

The growth of American pleasure boating is perhaps best illustrated by the incredible number of small, stock cruising sailboats now available. For instance, a purchaser seeking a cruiser-racer 30′ or less overall, with four permanent berths, galley, and head, would have approximately 170 stock models to choose from, ranging in size down to 17 feet.

How to define a small sailing cruiser? The Midget Ocean Racing Club has set 30′ LOA as their limit, and insists further on at least two berths, minimal galley, and head. For most people, four berths—or, more accurately, sleeping spaces for four adults—seems to be a necessity, albeit a largely psychological one.

Galley is a vague term by itself. In the past small shelves have been tucked in odd corners, labeled *galley* on the plans, and the boats containing them sent forth as legitimate cruisers. For most of us, a galley-equipped boat is one that has at least the space for a stove, sink (with water supply), and icebox. Some or all of these items may well be optional extras, and in very small cruisers, the several elements of the galley may be quite spread out. Iceboxes, for example, often wind up in the cockpit; when one stops to consider the realities of cruising, a cockpit-located icebox is very handy much of the time, although it does lead to bloat among the crew. On some boats, you can have it both ways, with an icebox opening both into the cockpit and down below.

Where you spend your time aboard is something that's too often forgotten: in most parts of the United States, sailing is an outdoor activity, and boats that sacrifice cockpit space to accommodation are bound to be unsatisfactory, no matter how cute

they may appear on the showroom floor.

Offshore racers' cockpits are generally rather small, by cruising standards: a racer's cockpit, after all, is designed to contain a working crew in an orderly fashion, while not encouraging too much water from a breaking wave. A cruiser uses his boat's cockpit for playpen, outdoor living room, and sprawl space—and sometimes as extra sleeping area as well.

As for the racing potential of a given boat, it will depend on so many variables that it's hard to pin down, except by citing the successful models, many of which are partially outdated by the time their fame has spread. Even the most devoted cruiser should not totally ignore racing requirements, because sooner or later he'll be overcome (even if only momentarily) with the urge to win, and he'll be sorely disappointed if his boat is simply out of the question.

Character boats aside, however, nearly all current, stock boats have some racing potential, as well as reasonable accommodations. A boat's racing chances depend not only on her (and your) absolute attributes, but also on the type of fleet in which she'll be competing. My own Bermuda-30, for instance, than which a slower boat would be hard to find, could compete with reasonable success in the sail fleet of the local Power Squadron: the other boats range from yesterday's MORC hero to a Herreshoff yawl that's well over the half-century mark, and the simplified, local rating system is correspondingly understanding.

What to look for in this size boat thus depends—as always—on your aim. There are, however, a few possible pointers (often learned the hard way) that may be helpful.

1. Don't expect perfection: if this is your first or second sailboat, it almost certainly won't be your last. Make, if you can, an honest assessment of what you really expect the boat to provide, and pick the boat to fit the bill. Unless silverware or practicality are the final considerations, don't buy a boat you privately consider ugly: a boat is a thing to love, and it's hard to summon up true affection for a 19.3 MORC rating. At the same time, unless you have some special requirements, stay away from freak boats: much as you love her now, cold statistics say you'll put her on the block in a couple of years, and how much will other buyers agree with you then?

2. Number of berths: as noted above, most people seem to want at least four. A safe way of deciding is to consider the true number of berths required—how many of you are going to sail regularly? how many to work the boat in a race?—and then accept additional berths only if they are also suitable for additional stowage. While you can find MORC boats that will sleep as many as eight, be sure you want what that implies: not eight motionless mummies, but eight snoring, writhing humans, trying simultaneously to don eight sets of clothing at once.

As to type of berths, that will vary with the use: a racer's berths should be fairly narrow —no more than 24″—and well bunkboarded against ejection of occupant when the boat heels. On a pure cruiser, where most sleeping is done at anchor, the best berths are simply the biggest ones—for sleeping: when the same berths have to function as seats during dinner, width isn't as desirable. Look for berths with some form of removable backrest to achieve the best compromise.

Foam mattresses should be at least 3″ thick over a hard surface, and the covering material is a matter of personal opinion: duck or standard fabric stains easily and dries slowly, but it's more comfortable to many tender skins than the clammy embrace of plain vinyl. If upper berths are in your picture, don't shun the so-called Root berth or canvas cot: properly laced canvas can be quite comfortable to sleep on.

3. A workable galley: no matter how ingenious the designer, it's not going to be a ranchhouse kitchen. Again, what will be tolerable will depend on the kinds of meals you plan to produce. A gimballed, two-burner pressure stove can (with a little pre-planning) provide adequate hot meals under way for four hungry people. But a single burner is far less than half as useful, because it will be immobilized so much of the time by the boiling of water. The amount of water boiled on the average small cruiser suggests that a country doctor (played by Paul Muni) is up in the fore-peak, delivering quints.

For any kind of genuine usefulness, your racer-cruiser's icebox should be capable of handling a 50-pound block of ice, two or three six-packs of life-giving fluid (your choice), a quart container of milk, a pound of butter, miscellaneous glass jars to the number of half a dozen, and perhaps a main dish or two in frozen form. If you're considering a foreign-built boat, make sure the icebox is properly insulated and conveniently located: foreign boatbuilders have all heard about the American mania for ice with everything, but they don't entirely believe it, and their iceboxes are often dry food lockers with an extra-thick door.

Stowage of non-refrigerated foods can be considerably less of a problem, as long as the containers won't break or melt. Just remember, though, that if you use odd corners of the boat for food storage, you should have an updated list of what's where: in winter, the whole boat may be abruptly refrigerated by Mother Nature, and a tin of soda can create an appalling mess when it explodes.

4. Stowage generally: the marine version of Parkinson's Law reads, "Vital gear to be stowed on any small boat equals 1.2 of the area available to stow it in." One of the penalties of mass production is the absence of all those clever hand-carpentered lockers found on older boats. But half those little cubbies were too small for anything bigger than a stack of dimes, and the costs of including too much handwork in a fiberglass boat are simply prohibitive—to me and you, as well as the manufacturer.

The handy owner can double the stowage capabilities of nearly any boat. For small boats, pullman-style hammocks will not only hold a lot of clothing but will also keep it ventilated, which is a necessity if you plan to be out more than a weekend.

A hanging locker isn't the necessity it was when foul weather gear, folded wet, would vulcanize itself into rigor mortis. Still, a hanging locker is nice to have—but it doesn't have to be the height of your hall closet: a jacket on a hanger (wood or plastic) requires only two and a half or three feet of vertical space.

Quarter berths under the cockpit seat lockers make good temporary stowage areas, too—especially for bedding, which is always a problem in daytime. In some cases, quarter berths are accessible from the cockpit as well as the cabin, which means that little people can sleep in the forward half, and the after part can be saved for coils of line, fenders, and the like.

5. The key word is *headroom*: like many key words, however, its meaning and necessity depend on who's doing the talking. In a boat under 24 feet or so, it's very difficult to have full standing headroom below for the average adult male—if you define said headroom as six feet. There are a number of boats that offer 5'8" or 5'9", and a gallant skipper with a mini-wife may calculate that headroom for some of the family at least is better than none.

Others will find not-quite-standing headroom purely maddening, and prefer stooping constantly in return for the decreased windage (and increased performance) to be obtained from a small boat without a high doghouse. It's a perfectly reasonable view (as Philip L. Rhodes has said, "You don't have standing headroom in a Cadillac"), and as long as there's full, sitting headroom—about 54"—the cabin can be quite bearable.

6. How much will she cost? How high is up? Boat prices are almost infinitely variable, depending on owners' whims, and those pertaining to this intermediate size craft are exceptionally elastic, primarily because most of these vessels are suitable for either outboard or inboard power, and the various lighting and generating complications arising from this decision. Between outboard and inboard, there can be a price difference for the same boat of a thousand dollars or two. Even an outboard-powered boat, in the middle of this size range, can chew the best part out of a ten-thousand dollar bill, and the sails alone in a 30 footer can cost over $1,200, plus another $500 for spinnaker and genoa gear.

The important thing to remember, buying a new boat, is to add up *all* of what you'll need before you start thinking of her as costing X dollars. But there's a bright note to the financial picture: the sailor of a few years back could spend the same amount only to find his wood boat had depreciated tremendously at the end of a couple of years. Today's skipper, with his 'glass boat, Dacron sails, and alloy spars, can have confidence that his investment will remain in good order for some time to come.

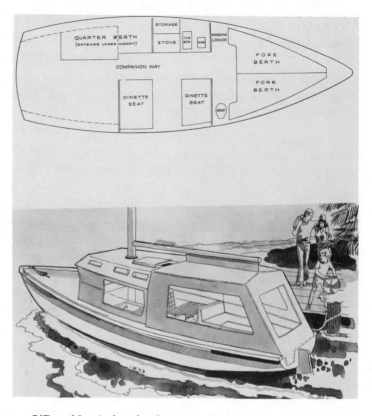

Kittiwake—A minimum four-berth cruiser.
LOA 23'7" / LWL 17'9" / Beam 7'5" / Draft 2'10" / Sail Area 248 sq. ft. / Displacement 3,700 lbs.

O'Day 23—A four-berth camper type cruiser which has full headroom with the cabin top raised.
LOA 23'1" / LWL 20' / Beam 7'11" / Draft 2'-5'5" / Sail Area 245 sq. ft.

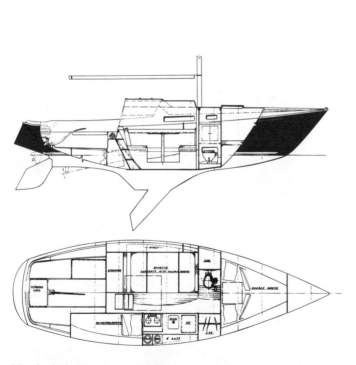

Northwind 29—A successful keel-centerboard sloop with raised deck.
LOA 28'9½" / LWL 22' / Beam 9'2" / Draft 3'1"-6'9" / Sail area 374 sq. ft. Displacement, 6,193 lbs.

Arpege—profile and interior layout of a popular cruiser from France.
LOA 30'4" / LWL 22' / Beam 9'11" / Draft 4'5" / Sail Area 399 sq. ft. / Displacement

33: The Well-Found Boat

Part of a skipper's responsibility is deciding how best to fit out his vessel to make her *well-found*—equipped and maintained to meet the conditions she'll encounter.

There are basically two ways of deciding what gear a boat should carry. First is the objective approach: set up certain classes of vessels, based on some visible standard like overall length, and graduate the equipment to suit the size of craft. The second method is to equip the boat, whatever its size, in terms of its projected use. Each of these systems has its defects, and the wise skipper will combine the best features of both methods.

Below are three tables; the first lists equipment required by Federal Law (the Motorboat Act of 1940 and subsequent amendments) for any pleasure boat 65′ or less equipped with a motor—which these days includes most sailboats; if you own a sailboat without a motor, you're exempt from the requirements of Federal law—*but* your state may have its own equipment regulations: check with the state boating authority.

Table Two indicates suggested equipment where it can be related to a boat's overall length; none of this gear is required by law, but much of it is mandatory out of simplest common sense.

Table Three deals with gear whose usefulness is related to a boat's intended service rather than to its length or to legal requirements. Do bear in mind, however, that service is at least partly related to size: what's open water to a 15 footer is close inshore to a 40′ ocean racer.

TABLE ONE: EQUIPMENT REQUIRED AS OF OCTOBER 1, 1978

Minimum Required Equipment

EQUIPMENT	CLASS A (Less than 16 feet)	CLASS 1 (16 feet to less than 26 feet)	Class 2 (26 feet to less than 40 feet)	CLASS 3 (40 feet to not more than 65 feet)
BACK-FIRE FLAME ARRESTER	One approved device on each carburetor of all gasoline engines installed after April 25, 1940, except outboard motors.			
VENTILATION	At least two ventilator ducts fitted with cowls or their equivalent for the purpose of properly and efficiently ventilating the bilges of every engine and fuel-tank compartment of boats constructed or decked over after April 25, 1940, using gasoline or other fuel of a flashpoint less than 110° F.			
BELL	None.*	None.*	One, which when struck, produces a clear, bell-like tone of full round characteristics.	
PERSONAL FLOTATION DEVICES	One Type I, II, III, or IV for each person.	One Type I, II, or III for each person on board or being towed on water skiis, etc., plus one Type IV available to be thrown.		
WHISTLE	None.*	One hand, mouth, or power operated, audible at least ½ mile.	One hand or power operated, audible at least 1 mile.	One power operated, audible at least 1 mile.
FIRE EXTINGUISHER— PORTABLE — When NO fixed fire extinguishing system is installed in machinery space(s).	At least One B–1 type approved hand portable fire extinguisher. (Not required on outboard motorboat less than 26 feet in length and not carrying passengers for hire if the construction of such motorboats will not permit the entrapment of explosive or flammable gases or vapors.)		At least Two B–1 type approved hand portable fire extinguishers; OR At least One B–11 type approved hand portable fire extinguisher.	At least Three B–1 type approved hand portable fire extinguishers; Or At least One B–1 type *Plus* One B–11 type approved hand portable fire extinguisher.
When fixed fire extinguishing system is installed in machinery space(s).	None.	None.	At least One B–1 type approved hand portable fire extinguisher.	At least Two B–1 type approved hand portable fire extinguishers; OR At least One B–11 type approved hand portable fire extinguisher.
	Note: Dry Chemical and Carbon Dioxide (CO_2) are the most widely used types, in that order. The others, while acceptable, are seldom seen on boats.			
	Fire extinguishers manufactured after 1 January 1965 will be marked, "Marine Type USCG Type ——— Size ——— Approval No. 162.028/EX . . ."**			

* NOTE.—Not required by the Motorboat Act of 1940; however, the "Rules of the Road" require these vessels to sound proper signals.

**NOTE.—Toxic vaporizing-liquid type fire extinguishers, such as those containing carbon tetrachloride or chlorobromomethane, are not accepted as required approved extinguishers on uninspected vessels (private pleasure craft).

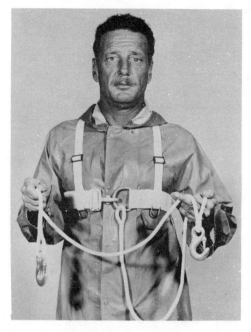

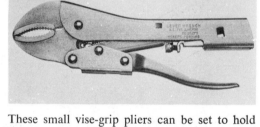

Typical small marine first aid kit. Skippers should familiarize themselves with such devices as the Resusitube before emergencies arise.

A good safety harness, like the one here, can be adjusted to fit the occupant. Note the oversize hardware and double snaphooks.

Diaphragm-type pumps like this have great capacity, seldom jam, and can be easily opened for inspection.

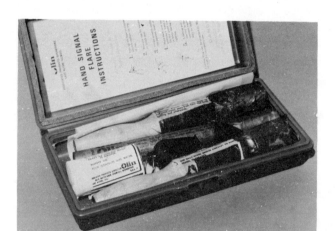

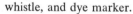

For most small craft this distress signal kit will be wholly adequate. It contains hand-held flares, orange smoke signal, whistle, and dye marker.

These small vise-grip pliers can be set to hold firm even after they have been released.

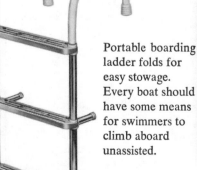

Portable boarding ladder folds for easy stowage. Every boat should have some means for swimmers to climb aboard unassisted.

A radio direction finder. This one also has an integral compass.

A hand-held anemometer is sufficient for most skippers. It will not, however, measure the wind at the masthead, which may be a good deal stronger than at deck level.

ADDITIONAL SAFETY AND OPERATIONAL EQUIPMENT, TABLE TWO: BY BOAT LENGTH

EQUIPMENT	CLASS A (to 16 feet)	CLASS 1 (16 feet to 26 feet)	CLASS 2 (26 feet to 40 feet)	CLASS 3 (40 feet to 65 feet)
Anchor and line	One suitable for local waters.	At least two—one heavy, one light—with suitable lines.		Three: heavy, medium, light, with rodes.
Bilge blower	Highly desirable for inboard boats of all sizes.			
Boathook	Desirable. The telescoping type takes little stowage space.		A solid one at least 8 feet long.	
Bosun chair		If mast is strong.	Vital.	
Cockpit awning		Vital in hot climates, very nice to have elsewhere.		
Depth Sounder		Useful.	Important.	Vital.
Dinghy		Maybe an inflatable.	Nice to vital.	Essential.
Ditty bag	For every sailboat:	see Chapter 27.		
Dock lines	At least two.	At least four.		Six or more, plus a long spare for towing.
Fenders	At least two.	Two or three oversize, plus a fenderboard if boat is frequently rafted.		Four large ones, plus a fenderboard.
Fume detector		Nothing really beats your nose, but larger sailing auxiliaries have some pretty unreachable corners where fumes can collect.		
Handy billy		A portable purchase, useful in many situations.		
Heaving line			Nice but not vital.	Desirable.
Navigation lights	Portable, if any.	Portable or permanent.	Portable or permanent; anchor light should be independent of main power supply.	
Oars or paddles	Pair.	If usable.		
Spotlight	One or more portable, waterproof lights, in addition to waterproof flashlight.			
Spare parts	Engine parts (see manufacturer's recommendations), extra slides and sail snaps, battens (one of each size), shackles, cotter pins or rings, batteries, turnbuckle, shock cord, snap shackles.			
Swimming ladder	Some way to get a tired person into the boat from the water is vital.			
Tools	In addition to engine tools, sailors usually carry a knife, marlinspike, visegrip pliers—plus tools for rope-work, in your ditty bag.			

TABLE THREE: BY BOAT SERVICE

EQUIPMENT	INSHORE	SEMI-PROTECTED	OPEN WATER
Charts and navigator's tools	Local charts.	Charts plus dividers, protractor, cruise guide, tide and current tables.	Same, plus stop watch, range finder, light list.
Compass	Portable, damped.	Fixed marine type.	Same, plus hand bearing compass.
Distress signals	Hand-held flares, orange smoke, distress flag.		Same, plus flare gun, dye markers.
Diving gear	Fins and mask are useful for in-service bottom cleaning.		
Emergency food and water	If space allows.	One day's supply.	In proportion to crew and voyage.
Fire extinguisher (extra)	At least one B–1 size for every living compartment.		
First Aid Kit	Small commercial type.	Larger commercial type.	Ask your physician to add extra items for long cruises and/or known crew ailments.
Instruments	Hand-held anemometer, barometer should be adequate.	Same, plus speedometer.	Masthead anemometer plus apparent wind indicator, speedometer and/or log.
Life raft		Required by racing organizations—useful to vital, depending on size of dinghy.	
Life ring/horseshoe		Useful, especially with waterlight and whistle attached. Required for most distance races.	
Propeller (spare)		Good to have.	Important.
Pulpit/lifelines	Through-bolted pulpit and stanchions, with plastic-coated wire lines, useful for any boat where crew can work on deck. Required for offshore work.		
Pump	At least one.		Two, one of which is manual.
RDF		Occasionally useful.	Often useful.
Radio	Receiver, for weather reports.	Same, plus VHF transmitter	Plus marine band transmitter.
Rigging cutters		Required for distance races.	
Safety harnesses		Required for distance races; sized to fit crew.	
Sea anchor			Useful.
Spreader lights		Nice to have at night for sail changing.	
Tiller (spare)		Vital for wheel-steered boat or offshore service.	

34: Money Matters

How much your sailboat will cost depends to a great extent on how much you can afford to spend—and only you and the IRS know what that is. There are, however, two basic points to keep in mind.

First (assuming you are one of those organized people who can establish a budget and live with it) is the decision as to what portion of your recreational dollar boating will take. If yours is one of the many families who find their boat a way of life, you needn't set aside other parts of your disposable income for ski trips or country club memberships. If, on the other hand, your boating is only part of an overall recreational picture of some complexity, you'll want to keep your expenditures on the water in line with that aim.

Second, bear in mind that the cost of your boat is the combined amount of her price and her maintenance (less, eventually, her resale value). Skippers who feel that their expenses are over once they have paid the builder are likely to be continually overextended, especially at haulout and launching times. In addition, the man plagued by continual, unexpected charges will very likely develop a nagging sense of dissatisfaction—and that's certainly not the point of owning a boat.

Purchase Price

While many boats are sold in *sailaway condition,* practically none is truly complete, for the simple reason that complete is the owner's state of mind, not the builder's. (One of the facts of boating is that no boat is ever complete—there's always that one little thing yet to do.)

Some types of boat have been relatively standardized as to equipment, but in many —especially cruising/racing sailboats— owners have retained a pride in equipment selection that makes them want to pick nearly everything aboard. You can buy boats either way, but when figuring out the purchase price, be sure you know what will still have to be bought afterwards. If you make a general equipment list with prices, you can check with relative ease against the manufacturer's list of standard equipment to see what you'll have to buy.

And don't neglect the builder's optional extras: in many cases, he can supply it installed for what it would cost you before installation, especially in the case of gear requiring wiring or plumbing.

Financing

You said the fatal word—*Yes*—and the next thing that'll occur to you is how to pay for her. The days of J. P. Morgan are gone forever, and everyone asks how much it costs. You can finance a boat in the same way you can borrow money for any other major purchase. In fact, you may be able to finance it more easily than a few years ago, because lending institutions have discovered that boat owners are good risks. The default rate on boat purchase loans is very low—lower than on any other hardgoods purchase. Partly it is the financial status of boat buyers, but it seems also to be the case that a skipper would rather have his TV, car, or appliance repossessed than lose his boat.

Interest rates on boat loans are as good— or as bad—as those on other secured loans, and the terms available usually exceed those on everything but home and aircraft loans. Any dealer of repute can arrange a loan for you, either through a bank or some commercial credit organization. You may well have other sources of cash open, and they are worth investigating.

Just bear in mind that the interest should be worked into your boat's operating budget, just as your mortgage payments are a part of the expenses of running your house.

Warranties and Service

Today's boats nearly all carry warranties of one sort or another, and so do many major equipment items. A warranty may be complete or partial, fully protective or loose and vague. While the terms and language are certainly important, what's probably most vital is the man or men who stand behind it —the manufacturer and his dealer.

A good dealer is a man whose first thought is to get your boat back in business when something goes wrong, a man who'll make the repair first and sort out the exact details later as fairly as he can. If you're honest with a dealer, and he in turn has the reputation of honesty back at the factory, chances are he'll have no trouble getting his claims honored.

It is, therefore, a triangular operation: like all service work, the manufacturer depends on his dealer, who depends on you—as you've depended on the manufacturer right at the start. Specifically, you expect him to exercise his responsibility to produce a sound, seaworthy boat that performs according to specifications, when proper maintenance is kept up.

The dealer's job is to deliver the boat in operating condition—having checked it out himself and made sure everything works— and to advise the owner of required maintenance schedules, procedures, and standards. Having exercised his responsibility to the owner upon delivery, he now represents the builder in seeing to it that conditions of the warranty have been lived up to before any claims are made.

But the owner and no one else must follow the maintenance schedule, or at least see to it that some competent person does so. If a defect turns up, the owner should immediately advise the dealer.

Now the ball is in the dealer's court: he must ascertain if the problem is a result of fair wear and tear, owner's negligence, or some other non-warranted cause, or if it is covered, and his—the dealer's—prime responsibility.

Some prior arrangement between dealer and builder will cover whether the boat is returned for repair or fixed by the dealer and the company billed. Given the size of the average boat, chances are it'll be repaired at the dealer's establishment, by him or someone sent out from the factory.

Getting the job done, once the responsibility has been determined, remains as difficult in the boating field as it is in plumbing and heating or appliance work ashore.

There are simply not enough skilled workmen to meet rising demands, especially in a seasonal business like boating.

Needless to say, the dealer who values you as a continued customer, one who can be expected to come back again and again, will be most interested in keeping you a happy client. More and more boat dealers are realizing that a boat—most particularly a first boat—is a very periodic purchase, and that present owners are tomorrow's customers.

Not all dealers have perceived this, and service does remain a problem. Until the milennium, the buyer's best course of action is to do a little earwork: most boat owners who are happy with their dealer-skipper relationship will talk your ear off about it. A good dealer is widely known in his area, and sometimes well beyond it, and word of mouth is a quite reliable guide.

Insurance

There are any number of insurance policies for boats, and many smaller craft are covered, wholly or in part, by homeowners' policies. If your boat is Class A or 1 in size, it's worth while checking this with your regular insurance agent.

Larger boats are generally the subject of individual policies which take into account the hazards peculiar to the sea. Whatever the particular policy, there are two general areas of coverage. First is hull insurance— damage to, or destruction of, the boat herself. Second is liability, which insures you against the consequences of damaging other boats, people, or things.

Hull insurance obviously covers far more than the boat's hull alone; as usually written, in fact, it covers everything aboard, and protects you against fire, theft, the several types of common marine accidents, and sometimes (in older policies) against some fairly exotic hazards as well. Hull insurance is not cheap, and ranks as a major —if predictable—annual expense. With some companies, certain high equipment standards, or evidence on your part of nautical accomplishment (advanced USPS courses successfully taken, for instance), may entitle you to a reduced rate. It is only fair to say, however, that marine insurance rates have been increasing steadily in the past few years.

It is important to know the precise limitations of your policy, and these fall into three general areas: time, place, and activity. That is to say, your policy probably allows you to keep your boat in commission from date X in the spring to date Y in the fall, after which it must be stored ashore; your geographic limits of navigation are specified; and coverage is reduced or eliminated if the boat engages in certain forms of activity—racing is a prime example, especially as applied to coverage on sails and spars.

The limits of navigation are, for most skippers, wildly generous. It is, however, important to observe the time limits on keeping the boat in commission. If you want extra time in the water, just advise the agent in advance—the charges, if any, are trifling.

As with warranties, a good agent representing a good company is your best guarantee of attentive, careful service. For most cruising boats, a company specializing in marine insurance is indicated.

Running Expenses

Thanks to the proliferation of almanac-type boating guides, you may now be able to make an annual survey of local mooring and storing charges without leaving your house. These are generally made on a basis of boat length, with occupancy of the berth (or yard space) for a given number of months. Traditionally, winter storage charges include hauling and launching, but not scrubbing the bottom, winterizing, or rigging. Some yards offer package prices, though, so the entry in the regional guidebook may not tell the whole story.

Likewise, docking fees should include electricity and water (assuming these conveniences are laid on in the first place). Until you have actually done it, the commissioning and decommissioning of a particular boat is very hard to budget. In fact, no one can tell you in advance what your annual expenses will come to.

One way of coming to grips with this essentially elusive situation is to establish a fund—perhaps in a separate savings account—for your boat's maintenance. The first year, flying more or less blind, you'll begin to get a feel of things. By the end of the second year, you should be able to budget most major expenses with reasonable accuracy—especially if you remember to feed the kitty a little extra for each major new sail or piece of mechanical gear.

The trouble is that by the time you've got the whole thing taped, you'll probably have that boat buying gleam in your eye again.

Appendix A

Running Lights

All boats should be prepared to operate after dark. For small sailboats, under 23 feet, and not under power, a bright flashlight or lantern will do. Over 23 feet, a sailboat must have a red and green light installed, either on the bow, on the masthead, or mounted separately on each side of the boat. Additionally, she must have a white stern light, and, when proceeding under power, a white 360° masthead light, too. A new option for a sailboat without the engine on is a red over green light on the mast. See Chapman's *Piloting* for further details.

Appendix B

Rules of the Road

The first thing most sailors learn about the nautical Rules of the Road is that sailboats have the right of way over powerboats. While this is generally true, it's not true all the time: when a sailboat is overtaking a powerboat, the powerboat has the right of way; and a sailboat has no right to hamper the passage of a powered vessel in a narrow channel, when the powered craft cannot navigate outside that channel.

When a sailboat is under power, or under both power and sail, she becomes a powerboat as far as the Rules of the Road and the lighting requirements are concerned. Since so many small sailboats carry some form of auxiliary motor, the wise sailboat skipper will be familiar with both power and sail Rules of the Road. The diagrams that follow illustrate the right-of-way rules under In-

land Rules for both sail and power craft. In waters covered by the International Rule, there's one important difference in the sail-to-sail rules: the *close-hauled and running free* situation is not covered by the International Rules. Boats in these waters thus observe either the starboard-tack over port-tack rule or the leeward over windward rule, whichever applies. The Great Lakes Rules of the Road, generally follow the Inland Rules.

Copies of the complete rules are available, free, from Commandant (CHS), U.S. Coast Guard, Washington, D.C. 20226. Both International and Inland rules are contained in the same book, CG-169; Great Lakes Rules are in CG-172, and Western Rivers Rules (the Mississippi system) are contained in CG-184.

Appendix B

INLAND RULES OF THE ROAD – SAIL

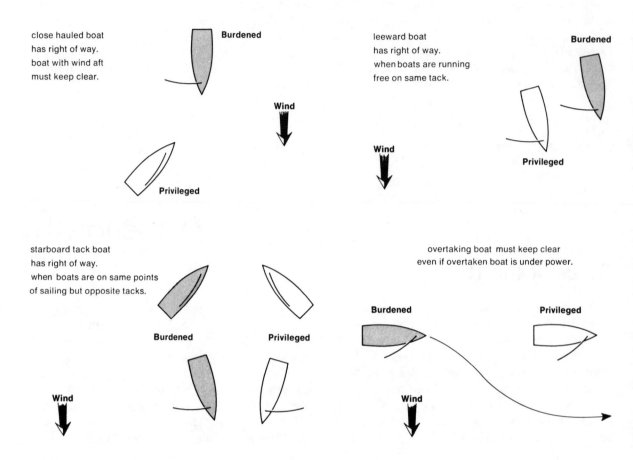

close hauled boat
has right of way.
boat with wind aft
must keep clear.

Burdened

Wind

Privileged

leeward boat
has right of way.
when boats are running
free on same tack.

Burdened

Wind

Privileged

starboard tack boat
has right of way.
when boats are on same points
of sailing but opposite tacks.

Burdened

Privileged

Wind

overtaking boat must keep clear
even if overtaken boat is under power.

Burdened

Privileged

Wind

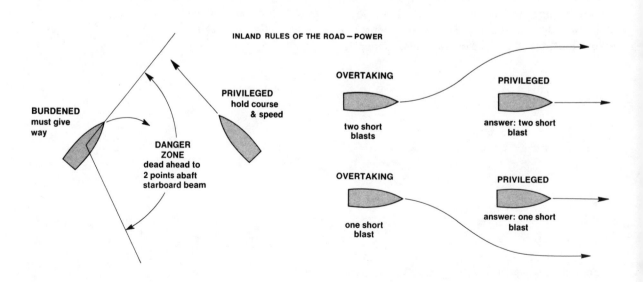

INLAND RULES OF THE ROAD – POWER

BURDENED
must give
way

PRIVILEGED
hold course
& speed

**DANGER
ZONE**
dead ahead to
2 points abaft
starboard beam

OVERTAKING

two short
blasts

PRIVILEGED

answer: two short
blast

OVERTAKING

one short
blast

PRIVILEGED

answer: one short
blast

Glossary A-B

ABAFT—farther toward the stern: the mizzen-mast is *abaft* the mainmast.

ABEAM—at right angles to the centerline of the boat, but not on the boat.

ABOARD—on or in the boat.

ADRIFT—orig.: loose from its moorings; hence, not made fast to any stationary object.

AFT—near, or toward, the stern of a boat.

AGROUND—touching or stuck on the bottom.

AHEAD—in the direction of, and forward of, the bow.

AHOY—term used in hailing a boat (archaic).

ALEE—away from the direction of the wind, usually referring to movement of the helm or tiller.

ALOFT—above the deck, usually in the rigging.

AMIDSHIPS—center portion of a vessel between bow and stern; also portion of the vessel between port and starboard sides.

ANCHOR'S AWEIGH—said of the anchor when just broken free of the bottom.

ANCHORAGE—a place suitable for anchoring: usually, out of traffic, sheltered, with good *holding ground* (q.v.).

ARM—the part of a yachtsman's anchor extending outward from the crown, and terminating in the fluke.

ASTERN—in the direction of, and beyond, the stern; opposite of *ahead*.

ATHWARTSHIPS—at right angles to the centerline of a boat.

AUXILIARY—orig.: the small engine of a sailing craft; by extension, a sailboat with an auxiliary engine: an auxiliary.

B

BACK—the wind is said to *back* when it changes its direction counter-clockwise.

BACKSTAY(S)—standing rigging that supports the mast from aft: *standing backstay* runs from masthead to stern; *running backstays* are a pair of braces running aft from the mast to a point on either quarter, where they are adjusted by levers or winches.

BACKWIND—wind deflected off a boat's sail into the leeward side of another sail; one sail is thus said to *backwind* another.

BALLOON JIB, BALLOONER—a large headsail of great draft, used for reaching.

BARE POLES—a sailboat that is under way with no sail set: usually a heavy weather precaution —"the yacht bore off before the storm under bare poles."

Glossary B

BARGE—a cargo-carrying vessel, usually without an engine. Also a term in sail racing—a boat which forces its way illegally between another contestant and the starting line is said to be *barging*.

BATTEN DOWN—originally, to secure hatches with canvas covers, held in place by battens; hence, to prepare for a storm.

BEAM—the greatest width of a vessel.

BEAM REACH—sailing with the wind at right angles to the boat.

BEAR—to *bear down* is to approach from windward, to *bear off* is to sail away to leeward.

BEARING—the direction of an object, expressed either as a true bearing, or as a relative bearing: relative to some second object, usually one's own vessel.

BEAT—to sail to windward in a series of tacks. *Beating* is one of three points of sailing (see p. 23), also known as sailing *close-hauled* or *by the wind*.

BEAUFORT SCALE—a system of describing wind forces by numbers, from 0 for a flat calm to 12 for a hurricane.

BEFORE THE WIND—in the same direction the wind blows, as a point of sailing.

BELAY—to make fast a line to a cleat or belaying pin; also, to rescind an order which is being carried out.

BEND—a knot that fastens one line to another; also, to attach a sail to a spar.

BERTH—a sailor's bed; also, vessel's allotted place at a pier or marina.

BIGHT—any part of a rope between the ends, but usually a loop.

BILGE—the interior of the hull below the floorboards.

BINNACLE—a stand containing the steering compass.

BITT—vertical timber extending through the deck, to which lines are made fast.

BITTER END—the last part of a rope or final link of a chain.

BLANKET—a sail that is deprived of wind by an intervening sail or boat is said to be blanketed.

BLOCK—nautical word for pulley; blocks with a rope through them form a tackle.

BOARD—one tack of a series; often an uneven series composed of *long boards* and *short boards*.

BOLT ROPE—line stitched to the foot and luff of a sail to give it strength or to substitute for sail slides. (See p. 14)

BOOM—spar to which the foot of a sail is attached, and which is itself attached to the mast.

BOOM CROTCH OR CRUTCH—a notched board or X-shaped frame that supports the main boom when sail is not raised.

BOOM VANG—a tackle running between boom and deck which flattens the sail's curve by downward pull on the boom.

BOOT-TOPPING—painted line that indicates the waterline.

BOS'N'S CHAIR—plank seat made fast to a halyard, for a man to sit on while working aloft.

BOW—the forward part of a vessel.

BOWLINE—knot used to form a temporary eye or loop in the end of a line. (See p. 85)

BOWSPRIT—a spar extending forward of the bow and set into the deck, to support the headsails.

BRIGHTWORK—polished metal fittings or varnished woodwork.

BROACH—a boat broaches-to when, while running free, it swings out of control and beam-on to wind or sea.

BROAD REACH—sailing with the wind more or less over either quarter. (See p. 22)

BULKHEAD—a vertical partition separating parts of the boat.

BY THE LEE—running with the wind on the same side as the main boom; very dangerous, because it invites an accidental jibe. (See p. 28)

BUNK—a sailor's bed.

BY THE WIND—sailing close-hauled.

C

CABIN—the enclosed or decked-over living space of a boat.

CABLE—the anchor rope or chain; also an obsolete measurement of 100 fathoms, or 600 feet.

CAPSIZE—to turn over.

CARRY AWAY—to break free.

CAST OFF—to let go, especially to let go a line.

CATAMARAN—boat with twin hulls joined at the center.

CATBOAT—sailboat with a single mast, stepped far forward, and one sail.

CAULK, OR CALK—to fill the seams of a boat with a compound that prevents leakage.

CENTERBOARD—a plate or board that can be raised or lowered through a slot in the bottom of a boat. (See p. 5)

CENTER OF EFFORT, abbreviated CE—the center of wind pressure on a sail.

Glossary C-D

CHAFE—to wear a sail, spar, or line by rubbing it against something. This is prevented by installation of *chafing gear*; sacrificial coverings, usually of canvas or rubber, whch absorb the chafe.

CHAIN PLATE—metal strap bolted or fiberglassed to the side of a sailboat, to which a shroud or stay is attached.

CHEEK BLOCK—a block whose sheave is mounted against a spar.

CHINE—the line formed by the intersection of the side and bottom of a flat- or V-bottomed boat.

CHOCK—a U-shaped fairlead secured in or on a boat's rail, for anchor and mooring lines.

CLEAT—a horned fitting of wood or metal to which lines are made fast.

CLEW—the lower after corner of a sail.

CLOSE-HAULED—sailing as close as possible to the wind. (See p. 23)

CLOSE REACH—sailing with sheets eased and the wind forward of the beam. (See p. 22)

CLOVE HITCH—a way of fastening a line temporarily to a spar. (See p. 86)

COCKPIT—the well in a boat's deck from which the crew handles her operation. A self-bailing cockpit is one fitted with drains that allow water to run back into the sea.

COIL—to lay a line down in circular turns. (See p. 90)

COURSE—the direction steered by a vessel.

CORDAGE—a general term for all types of rope.

CRADLE—a wooden framework supporting a boat out of the water.

CRINGLE—a ring sewn into a sail through which a line can be passed.

CUDDY—a shelter cabin in a small boat.

CURRENT—the horizontal movement of water, caused by tide or wind, or both.

D

DAGGER BOARD—a type of centerboard that does not pivot but is raised and lowered vertically (See p. 5).

DINGHY—a small boat, usually designed to be carried as tender to a larger craft. May be rigged for sail.

DINK—nickname for dinghy.

DISPLACEMENT—the weight of water displaced by a floating vessel; hence, the weight of the vessel itself.

DITTY BAG—a small bag for a sailor's sewing kit and other tools relating to sails and rope. (See p. 89)

DOUSE—to lower sail quickly.

DOWNHAUL—tackle attached to the underside of the gooseneck, to tighten a sail's luff by pulling down on the boom. (See p. 38)

DOWNWIND—to leeward, away from the wind.

DOWSE—see Douse.

DRAFT—the depth of water to the lowest point of a vessel's keel.

E

EASE—to slacken.

EVEN KEEL—a boat is on an even keel when it is floating level.

EYE OF WIND—the direction from which the wind is coming.

EYE SPLICE—a permanent loop in the end of a rope. (See p. 87)

F

FAKE—a rope is faked down when it is coiled so that each coil, or fake, overlaps the one beneath, and the line is thus free to run. (Also *flake*)

FALL OFF—to let a boat's head turn away from the wind.

FAST—secure: to make something fast is to secure it.

FATHOM—six feet, usually seen as a measurement of depth on charts.

FENDER—a portable anti-chafe device, usually tubular, placed between a boat and a pier or another boat.

FIGURE-EIGHT KNOT—a stopper knot, to keep the bitter end of a line from running through a block. (See p. 85)

FISHERMAN'S BEND—a knot that connects the rode to the anchor. (See p. 85)

FLAKE—a full turn in a coil of rope; a method of laying out rope in figure-8s, to run freely; method of placing a sail in layers across a spar. (See p. 85)

FLATTEN-IN—to trim sheets more closely.

FLUKE—the palm of an anchor. (See p. 49)

FLY—a masthead wind pennant.

FOOT—the lower edge of a sail.

FORE AND AFT—in line with the keel.

FOREPEAK—a compartment in the very bow.

FORE-REACHING—the forward motion of a vessel that is luffing and in the process of coming about, or shooting a mooring.

Glossary F-G-H

FORESAIL—the sail set from a schooner's fore-mast.

FORESTAY—a stay below and aft of the jib-stay on a yacht carrying two headsails.

FORWARD—toward the bow.

FOULED—jammed or entangled: not clear. Said of any piece of equipment.

FREEBOARD—the vertical distance from the waterline to the gunwale.

FULL AND BY—close hauled.

G

GAFF—a spar supporting the head of a four-sided, fore-and-aft sail. (See p. 16)

GASKET—a sail stop.

GHOST—a sailboat moving in little or no wind is said to be ghosting.

GO ABOUT—same as come about.

GOOSENECK—the moveable fitting connecting mast and boom. (See p. 10)

GROUND TACKLE—collective term for anchor and associated gear: cable, chain, swivel, etc.

GUNWALE—pronounced *gunnel*—the upper edge of a boat's side.

H

HALYARD—line or wire used for hoisting sails. (See p. 12)

HAND OVER HAND—way of gathering a line or multi-part tackle in short lengths. (See p. 30)

HARD ALEE (spelled in various ways)—the command given to put the boat about, by pushing the tiller to leeward.

HEADSAILS—sails forward of the foremost mast; includes jibs, genoas, spinnakers and spinnaker staysails.

HEAD UP—to head into the wind.

HEADWAY—boat's forward momentum.

HEAD—the upper corner of a triangular sail (see p. 13) or upper edge of a gaff sail. (See p. 16)

HEEL—to tip to one side.

HELM—the tiller or wheel. The man steering is thus the helmsman.

HITCH—properly, a method of making a rope fast to another rope or to a spar.

HOGGED—said of a boat whose bow and stern have sagged.

I

IN IRONS—stuck midway through coming about. (See p. 25)

IN STAYS—in irons.

IRISH PENNANT—frayed end of a rope.

J

JIB—triangular sail set ahead of the foremost mast. (See p. 16)

JIBE—to bring the wind to the opposite side of the boat when sailing with the wind aft, by turning the stern across the wind (See p. 28).

JIB SHEET—line controlling the jib. (See p. 16)

JIB STAY—stay running from bow or bowsprit to the mast, on which the jib is set. If the stay runs to the masthead, it may be called a head-stay.

JIGGER—the mizzen sail of a ketch or yawl.

JUMPER—stay on the upper forward part of the mast. (See p. 11)

K

KEEL—in a wood boat, the principal timber running fore and aft along the centerline, like the spine of a man. In fiberglass craft, the centerline itself.

KEEL BOAT—a boat with a fixed, ballast keel, as opposed to a centerboard boat.

KETCH—a two-masted sailboat in which the smaller aftermast—the mizzen—is stepped forward of the rudder post.

KNOCKDOWN—said of a boat that is laid over suddenly, by wind or sea, so that water pours over the gunwale. (See p. 78)

KNOT—a speed of one nautical mile (6080 feet) per hour. A knot is not a measure of distance, but of rate of speed.

L

LANYARD—a short line, usually attached to some piece of loose gear, for making it fast.

LAY—to lay a mark (see p. 30) is to be able to reach it in a single tack, close-hauled. The lay of a line is the direction in which its strands are twisted.

LAZARETTE—compartment for gear stowage at the stern of a boat.

LEECH—sometimes spelled *leach*—the after edge of a fore-and-aft sail.

LEEWARD—pronounced *loo*-ard, the direction away from the wind.

Glossary L-M-O-P

LEEWAY—drift to leeward. (See p. 30)

LEE HELM—a boat out of balance, so as to turn away from the wind when the helm is amidships, is said to carry lee helm (See p. 55).

LIGHT SAILS—sails made of extra-light material, such as the spinnaker and drifter.

LOCKER—a stowage compartment.

LONG SPLICE—a method of permanently joining the ends of two ropes without increasing the diameter.

LOOSE-FOOTED—said of a sail that secures to the boom at tack and clew only. (See p. 9)

LUFF—the forward edge of a sail; also, to head up into the wind, thus causing the sail to ripple.

M

MAINMAST—the principal mast of a boat.

MAINSAIL—the sail that sets abaft the mainmast. (See p. 14)

MAINSHEET—the sheet controlling the mainsail. (See p. 12)

MARLINSPIKE—a tool for opening the strands of a rope while splicing. (See p. 89)

MAST STEP—the shaped brace on which the butt of the mast rests. (See p. 9)

MIZZEN—the after and smaller mast of a ketch or yawl. Also the sail set on that mast.

MOORING—large anchor permanently (or seasonally) in place, to which is attached a line or chain with a buoy at the top. (See p. 49)

O

OFF THE WIND—sailing on a reach or run.

OUTBOARD—toward or beyond the boat's sides.

OUTHAUL—device for stretching the foot of a sail along the boom. (See p. 9)

P

PAINTER—dinghy towrope or dock line.

PAY OFF—to turn away from the wind.

PAY OUT—to ease out a line.

PINCH—to sail a boat closer to the wind than she can efficiently go.

POINT—ability to sail close to the wind (See p. 17). Also, $\frac{1}{32}$ of a circle ($11\frac{1}{4}°$).

PORT—the left side of a vessel, looking forward.

PORT TACK—sailing with the wind coming over a boat's port side. (See p. 25)

PREVENTER—a guy line led forward from the end of a boom or pole to keep it from accidentally swinging.

PUFF—a gust of wind.

Glossary Q-R-S

Q

QUARTER—the part of a boat lying within 45° of the stern; every boat thus has a starboard and a port quarter.

R

RAKE—the angle of a vessel's mast from the perpendicular.

REACH—the point of sailing between close-hauled and running. (See p. 22)

READY ABOUT—preparatory order given before, "Hard alee," to put the boat about.

REEF—to reduce the area of the sail. (See p. 72)

REEF POINTS—short lines set into the sail to aid in reefing.

REEVE—to pass a line through a block.

RIGGING—general term for the lines (wire and rope) that support the spars (standing rigging) and control the hoisting and set of the sails (running rigging). (See p. 10)

ROACH—the curve in the leech of a sail. (See p. 14)

RODE—anchor line.

ROLLING HITCH—a knot used when a lengthwise pull along a spar is required (See p. 86). Also may be secured to another line.

RUDDER—a steering device at the stern of a boat. (See p. 7)

RUNNING—sailing with the wind astern. (See p. 19)

RUNNING RIGGING—sheets, halyards, topping lifts, outhauls, etc. (See p. 10).

S

SCULLING—moving the tiller rapidly back and forth to move the boat ahead. Illegal in racing. Also a method of propelling a small boat with a single oar at the stern.

SEA ROOM—safe distance from the shore or other hazards.

SEAWORTHY—said of a boat or boat's gear in fit condition to meet the sea.

SECURE—to make fast.

SEIZE—to bind with a thin line. (See p. 86)

SHACKLE—a U-shaped connector with a removable pin.

SHEAVE—the grooved wheel in a block.

SHEET—the line used to trim a sail.

SHEET BEND—a knot used to join two ropes.

SHROUD—standing rigging that supports a mast athwartships. (See p. 11)

SHORT SPLICE—a method of permanently joining two ropes' ends. (See p. 89)

Glossary S-T

SLACK—not fastened; loose. Also, to loosen.

SLOOP—single-masted sailboat whose working sails are main and jib.

SNATCH BLOCK—a block that opens at the side, so a bight of line can be inserted or removed without reeving the entire line through.

SPARS—general term for masts, booms, gaffs, etc., which have in common that they hold sails extended.

SPINNAKER—a light weather headsail used in running and reaching. (See p. 60)

SPLICE—to permanently join two lines by tucking their strands alternately over and under each other. (See p. 87)

SQUALL—sudden, violent gust of wind, often accompanied by rain.

SQUARE KNOT—a knot used to join two lines of similar size. Also called a reef knot. (See p. 85)

STANDING PART—the part of a rope that is made fast.

STANDING RIGGING—shrouds and stays supporting the mast. (See p. 10)

STARBOARD—the right side of a vessel, facing forward.

STARBOARD TACK—sailing with the wind coming over a boat's starboard side. (See p. 25)

STAY—rigging supporting the mast from forward or aft. (See p. 10)

STAYSAIL—name for several types of sail having the luff secured to a stay.

STEERAGEWAY—enough motion for the rudder to be effective. (See p. 42)

STEM—the bow of a boat.

STERN—the after part of a boat.

STOCK—the crossbar of an anchor. (See p. 49)

STOP—strap, piece of line, or length of shock cord used to lash a furled sail. (See p. 39)

STORM JIB—a very small jib set in heavy weather.

STOW—to put in place.

SWAMP—to fill a boat with water.

T

TABERNACLE—a hinge at the base of the mast, so that this spar can easily be lowered.

TACK—to come about (see p. 25); the lower, forward corner of the sail (see p. 13); sailing with the wind on one or the other side of the boat (see p. 25).

TACKLE—a purchase made up of blocks and line. (See p. 12)

TELLTALE—a wind direction indicator made of a bit of cloth, or other light material, tied to a shroud. (See p. 18)

THWARTS—seats in a boat.

THWARTSHIPS (also *athwartships*)—at right angles to a boat's centerline.

TILLER—the lever with which the rudder is turned. (See p. 7)

TOPPING LIFT—adjustable line from the masthead supporting a boom.

TRAVELLER—an athwartships track or bar on which the mainsheet is led.

TURNBUCKLE—a tensioning device used with shrouds and stays. (See p. 11)

U

UNDER WAY—said of a boat in motion and under control.

UNREEVE—to run a line completely through and out of a block.

UP HELM—pushing the tiller toward the wind.

V

VANG—(See *boom vang*).

W

WAKE—a vessel's visible track through the water.

WAY ON—moving through the water, a boat is said to have way on.

WEATHER—the windward side.

WEATHER HELM—opposite of lee helm; the tendency of a boat with its rudder amidships to turn by itself to windward. (See p. 55)

WHIPPING—method of keeping a rope's end from unlaying. (See p. 87)

WIND'S EYE—the exact direction from which the wind is coming.

WINDWARD—the general direction from which the wind is coming.

Y

YAWL—a two-masted vessel whose small mizzen is stepped abaft the rudder post.